Breaking Through

Sequel to *The Circuit*

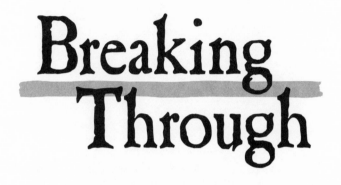

Breaking Through

Francisco Jiménez

Houghton Mifflin Company
Boston

To my family

© 2001 by Francisco Jiménez

www.houghtonmifflinbooks.com

The text of this book is set in 11-point Goudy.

Library of Congress Cataloging-in-Publication Data

Jiménez, Francisco, 1943–
Breaking through / Francisco Jiménez.
p. cm.
Sequel to: The circuit.
Summary: Having come from Mexico to California ten years ago, fourteen-year-old Francisco is still working in the fields but fighting to improve his life and complete his education.
ISBN 0-618-01173-0
1. Mexican Americans—Juvenile literature. [1. Mexican Americans—Biography. 2. Agricultural laborers—literature. 3. California—literature.] I. Title.
PZ7.J57525 Br 2001   [Fic]—dc21   2001016941

Manufactured in the United States of America
QUM 10 9 8 7 6 5 4 3

Acknowledgments

I would like to thank my brother, Roberto, and my mother, Joaquina, for providing me with a wealth of personal stories, some of which I have incorporated in this book. Special thanks to my immediate family—Laura, Pancho, Lori, Carlo Vicente, Miguel, and Tomás—for patiently listening to various drafts and offering helpful comments.

I wish to thank the community of my childhood, whose courage, tenacity, faith, and hope in the midst of adversity have been a constant inspiration to me in my writing and in my personal and professional life.

I have lasting gratitude to my teachers, whose guidance and faith in my ability helped me break through many barriers.

Thanks to many students, colleagues, and friends, especially Fr. Paul Locatelli, S.J., Fr. Stephen Privett, S.J.,

Peter Facione, Don Dodson, Alma García, Susan Erickson, and Alan Bern, for encouraging me to continue writing.

I am thankful to Santa Clara University for giving me the time to write this book and for valuing my work.

Finally, I am also indebted to my editor, Ann Rider, for her valuable suggestions for improvement and her gentle encouragement to write from the heart.

Contents

There is at bottom only one problem in the world…
How does one break through?
How does one get into the open?
How does one burst the cocoon and become a butterfly?

—Thomas Mann, *Dr. Faustus*

Forced Out

I lived in constant fear for ten long years, from the time I was four until I was fourteen years old.

It all started back in the late 1940s when Papá, Mamá, my older brother, Roberto, and I left El Rancho Blanco, a small village nestled on barren, dry hills several miles north of Guadalajara, Jalisco, Mexico, and headed to California, hoping to leave our life of poverty behind. I remember how excited I was making the trip on a second-class train traveling north from Guadalajara to Mexicali. We traveled for two days and nights. When we arrived at the United States–Mexico border, Papá told us that we had to cross the barbed-wire fence without being seen by *la migra*, the immigration officers dressed in green uniforms. During the night we dug a hole underneath the wire wall and wiggled like snakes under it to the other side. "If anyone asks you where you were born," Papá said firmly, "tell them Colton, California. If *la migra* catches you, they'll send you back to Mexico." We were picked up by a woman whom Papá had contacted in Mexicali. She drove us, for a fee, to a tent labor camp on the outskirts of Guadalupe, a small town on the coast. From that day on, for the next ten years, while we traveled from place to place throughout California, following the crops and living in migrant labor camps, I feared being caught by the Border Patrol.

As I got older, my fear of being deported grew. I did not want to return to Mexico because I liked going to school, even though it was difficult for me, especially English class. I enjoyed learning, and I knew there was no school in El Rancho Blanco. Every year Roberto and I missed months of school to help Papá and Mamá work in the fields. We struggled to make ends meet, especially during the winter, when work was scarce. Things got worse when Papá began to have back problems and had trouble picking crops. Luckily, in the winter of 1957, Roberto found a part-time job working year-round as a janitor at Main Street Elementary School in Santa Maria, California.

We settled in Bonetti Ranch, where we had lived in army barracks off and on for the past few years. My brother's job and mine—thinning lettuce and picking carrots after school and on weekends—helped support our family. I was excited because we had finally settled in one place. We no longer had to move to Fresno at the end of every summer and miss school for two and a half months to pick grapes and cotton and live in army tents or old garages.

But what I feared most happened that same year. I was in my eighth-grade social studies class at El Camino Junior High School in Santa Maria. I was getting ready to recite the preamble to the Declaration of Independence, which our class had to memorize. I had worked hard at memorizing it and felt confident. While I waited for class to start, I sat at my desk and recited it silently one last time:

> *We hold these truths to be self-evident: that all*
> *men are created equal; that they are endowed*
> *by their creator with certain unalienable rights;*
> *that among these are life, liberty, and the pursuit*
> *of happiness . . .*

I was ready.

After the bell rang, Miss Ehlis, my English and social studies teacher, began to take roll. She was interrupted by a knock on the door. When she opened it, I saw the school principal and a man behind him. As soon as I saw the green uniform, I panicked. I felt like running, but my legs would not move. I trembled and could feel my heart pounding against my chest as though it too wanted to escape. My eyes blurred. Miss Ehlis and the officer walked up to me. "This is him," she said softly, placing her right hand on my shoulder.

"Are you Francisco Jiménez?" he asked firmly. His deep voice echoed in my ears.

"Yes," I responded, wiping my tears and looking down at his large, black shiny boots. At that point I wished I were someone else, someone with a different name. My teacher had a sad and pained look in her eyes. I followed the immigration officer out of the classroom and into his car marked BORDER PATROL. I climbed in the front seat, and we drove down Broadway to Santa Maria High School to pick up Roberto, who was in his sophomore year. As cars passed by, I slid lower in the seat and kept my head down. The officer parked the car in front of the school and asked me to wait for him while he went inside the administration building.

A few minutes later, the officer returned with Roberto following him. My brother's face was as white as a sheet. The officer asked me to climb into the back seat with Roberto. "*Nos agarraron, hermanito,*" Roberto said, quivering and putting his arm around my shoulder.

"Yes, they caught us," I repeated. I had never seen my brother so sad. Angry, I added in a whisper, "But it took them ten years." Roberto quickly directed my attention to the officer with a shift of his eyes and put his index finger to his lips, hushing me. The officer turned right on Main Street and headed toward Bonetti Ranch, passing familiar sites I figured I would never see again: Main Street Elementary School; Kress, the five-and-dime store; the Texaco gas station where we got our drinking water. I wondered if my friends at El Camino Junior High would miss me as much as I would miss them.

"Do you know who turned you in?" the officer asked, interrupting my thoughts.

"No," Roberto answered.

"It was one of your people," he said, chuckling.

I could not imagine whom it could have been. We never told anyone we were here illegally, not even our best friends. I looked at Roberto, hoping he knew the answer. My brother shrugged his shoulders. "Ask him who it was," I whispered.

"No, you ask him," he responded.

The officer, who wore large, dark green sunglasses, must have heard us, because he glanced at us through the rearview mirror and said, "Sorry, can't tell you his name."

When we arrived at Bonetti Ranch, a Border Patrol van was parked in front of our house, which was one of many dilapidated army barracks that Bonetti, the owner of the ranch, bought after the Second World War and rented to farm workers. My whole family was outside, standing by the patrol car. Mamá was sobbing and caressing Rubén, my youngest brother, and Rorra, my little sister. They hung on to Mamá's legs like two children who had just been found after being lost. Papá stood between my two younger brothers, Trampita and Torito. Both cried silently as Papá braced himself on their shoulders, trying to ease his back pain. Roberto and I climbed out of the car and joined them. The immigration officers, who towered over everyone, searched the ranch for other undocumented residents, but found none.

We were hauled into the Border Patrol van and driven to San Luis Obispo, the immigration headquarters. There we were asked endless questions and given papers to sign. Since Papá did not know English and Mamá understood only a little, Roberto translated for them. Papá showed them his green card, which Ito, the Japanese sharecropper for whom we picked strawberries, had helped him get years before. Mamá showed birth certificates for Trampita, Torito, Rorra, and Rubén, who were born in the United States. Mamá, Roberto, and I did not have documentation; we were the only ones being forced to leave. Mamá and Papá did not want to separate our family. They pleaded with the immigration officer in charge to allow us to stay a few more days so that we could leave the country together. The officer finally agreed and told us we could leave on a voluntary basis. He gave us three days to report to the U.S. immigration office at the border in Nogales, Arizona.

The next morning as we were getting ready for our trip back to Mexico, I went outside and watched the school bus pick up kids from the ranch. As it drove away, I felt empty inside and had a pain in my chest. I went back inside to help pack. Papá and Mamá were sitting at the kitchen table surrounded by my brothers and sister, who listened quietly as my parents discussed our trip. Papá took out the metal box in which he kept our savings and counted it. "We don't have much, but we'll have to live on the other side of the border with the little we have. Maybe it'll last us until we fix our papers and come back legally," he said.

"And with God's help, we will!" Mamá said. "There's no doubt."

"I am not that sure, but we'll try," Papá responded.

I was happy to hear Papá and Mamá say this. I relished the thought of returning to Santa Maria, going back to school, and not fearing *la migra* anymore. I knew Roberto felt the same. He had a sparkle in his eyes and a big smile.

Papá and Mamá decided to cross the border in Nogales because they had heard that the immigration office there was not as busy as the one in Tijuana or Mexicali. We packed a few belongings, stored the rest in our barrack, and left our *Carcachita*, our old jalopy, locked and parked in front. Joe and Espy, our next-door neighbors, drove us to the Greyhound bus station on North Broadway in Santa Maria. We bought our tickets to Nogales and boarded. Papá and Rorra sat across the aisle from Roberto and me. Torito and Trampita sat in front of us. Roberto closed his eyes and leaned his head back. Tears rolled down his cheeks. He puckered his lower lip and clenched his hands.

I placed my left arm over his shoulder and looked out the window. The gray sky threatened rain. A boy about my age waved good-bye to a couple sitting behind us. He reminded me of Miguelito, my best friend in the third grade in Corcoran. I missed him for a long time after he and his family moved from the same labor camp we lived in.

We left Santa Maria Valley, passing by acres and acres of strawberry, artichoke, and alfalfa fields. We went through small towns and cities I had never heard of. Once we entered Arizona, the green fields and rolling hills gave way to desert plains and rugged mountains. I enjoyed watching jackrabbits leap suddenly from the cover of desert shrubs, land beside our speeding bus, and bolt back into the brush. Trampita and Torito played a game to see who spotted the most rabbits, but Papá had to stop it because they started quarreling. Torito accused Trampita of seeing double and Trampita claimed Torito did not know how to count.

We went by adobe houses with no front yards and unpaved streets. Papá said they reminded him of places in Mexico. As we approached some foothills of large mountains, there were hundreds of cactuses. "Look, *viejo*," Mamá said, pointing out the window. "Those *nopales* look like poor men stretching out their arms in prayer."

"They look more like men in surrender," Papá said.

"How about those two?" she said.

"Which ones?" Papá asked. "The two tangled together? They look like two people in shock."

"No, *viejo*," she countered. "They look like two people hugging each other." Mamá continued pointing out other cactuses to Papá until he got tired and refused to respond.

We stopped at Tucson and continued on to Nogales. Distant mountains lined the route on either side for much of the way. They rose above for several thousand feet, looking like giant caterpillars crawling out of the ground. That night the rain came down in sheets. Raindrops pelted the window, making it hard to fall asleep.

After traveling for about twenty hours, we arrived, exhausted, at the Nogales, Arizona, bus station in the morning. We picked up our belongings and headed to the immigration and customs office, where we reported in. We had made the deadline. We were then escorted on foot across the border to the Mexican side of Nogales. The twin cities were separated by a tall chainlink fence. Grassland, mesquite, scattered low shrubs, and bare rocky soil surrounded both sides of the border. The sky was cloudless and the streets were bone-dry. We walked the unpaved streets along the fence, looking for a place to stay. We ran into barefoot children in tattered clothes rummaging through waste bins. I felt a knot in my throat. They reminded me of when we were living in Corcoran and would go into town in the evenings looking for food in the trash behind grocery stores.

We finally found a cheap, rundown motel on Campillo Street, a few blocks from the border. As Papá and Mamá checked in, I looked around the cramped office. Through the dirty window, I could see part of the overpass bridging the two Nogaleses and the chainlink fence separating the two cities. On the corner of the dark yellow counter, which came up to my chin, was a pile of discolored motel brochures held in place by three small rocks. The shape and color of the stones fascinated me. They looked like gold nuggets. I picked one of them up to examine it closely, but Mamá slapped my hand and told me to put it back. When no one was looking, I snatched one and put it in my pocket.

The motel room was small, like the cabins we lived in at the cotton labor camps. We took the sagging mattress off the bed and placed it on the worn yellow linoleum floor so Papá and Mamá could sleep on it. The rest of us went to bed on the box spring. That night I felt listless and had a hard time sleeping. I kept thinking about what I had done. The following morning, I went outside, holding the rock in my fist and wondering what to do. I thought of throwing it underneath the overpass, but I felt guilty and scared. I went back to the office and, pretending I was getting a brochure, put it back.

Every day after Mamá bought food for us from street vendors for our meals, she and Papá went to the immigration office to check on our petition for visas. Each time they went they were asked for more information. Papá sent a telegram to Fito, my cousin in Guadalajara, asking him to secure our birth certificates and to send them to us by mail. Four days after they arrived, we were scheduled to take a medical examination. We were issued a one-day pass to cross the U.S. border and take the examination at St. Joseph's Hospital, which was located a few blocks from the U.S. customs office. We checked in at the front desk and sat in the waiting room to be called. The room's walls were light green and the white floors were spotless, just like the uniforms worn by the nurses and doctors. The receptionist came out and handed us a Foreign Service, U.S. Medical Examination of Visa Applicants form. Roberto helped Mamá read the form's long list of diseases and check yes or no.

After waiting for several hours, we were finally called in by the nurse, who collected the forms. I was asked to go first. She took me to a small room and handed my papers to the doctor, who glanced at them and asked me to strip to my shorts. I looked at the nurse, feeling as though my face were on fire. "All clean, no lice," she said after running a fine comb through my hair. The doctor double-checked the list of diseases I had marked on the form earlier.

"Amebiasis, gonorrhea, syphilis, trachoma?"

"No," I responded.

"Tuberculosis?"

I recalled the *bracero* who everyone thought had tuberculosis. He picked strawberries with us one summer when we worked for Ito. We thought he had tuberculosis because he was skinny as a rail and often coughed blood. We called him *El Tuberculosis*. One day he got so sick at work that Ito took him back to the *bracero* camp. That was the last time we saw him.

"Tuberculosis?" the doctor repeated impatiently.

"No."

"Ringworm?" he asked, turning my body around to check my back.

"I had it many years ago," I said.

When I was in third grade, I noticed I had two red spots about the size of a quarter, one on the left side of my stomach and another on the back of my scalp. I showed them to Mamá and told her they itched. "The devil made these marks. That's why they're red," she said, not blinking an eye. When she saw I was about to cry, she hugged me and said, "I am kidding, Panchito, *es roña*. I'll take care of it." She rubbed the red spots with garlic every day, and within a couple of weeks they were gone. The strong smell not only got rid of the ringworm, but it also kept my schoolmates away. Whenever I came near them, they yelled, "You stink like a Mexican!" and sprinted away from me, holding their noses.

"Your back looks fine," the doctor said. I felt an itch in my scalp, but I did not dare scratch it. "What about mental conditions: feeble-mindedness, insanity, psychopathic personality, epilepsy, narcotic drug addiction, chronic alcoholism?"

"No," I said, not knowing what those words meant.

"What about physical defects?"

"None." I figured he did not believe me, because he had me stretch out my arms and walk across the room. He then had me sit on the edge of the examination table, and he tapped my knees with a flat-nosed rubber hammer. My knee jerked so hard that I almost kicked him on the chin. The nurse then checked my weight and height.

"A hundred pounds and four feet eleven inches. You're a bit small for your age," she declared.

It was not the first time I was told that. My classmates at El Camino Junior High School, where I was the smallest kid, reminded me of it every time they chose teams to play basketball during recess.

"You can get dressed now," she said. "We're done."

Roberto went in next. When he came out his face was as red as a beet. He looked like he had been in a fight. His hair was messy and his shirt was half tucked in. He and I compared notes and laughed nervously when we got to the part of undressing in front of the nurse. "*Que vergüenza,*" he said. Mamá's checkup took a lot longer than Roberto's or mine. She did not say a word about it and Roberto and I did not ask.

After waiting for several days, we were notified that

our petition for an immigrant visa had been approved. Papá, Mamá, Roberto, and I were beside ourselves when we got the news. We could not stop smiling. My younger brothers and sister did not understand what it all meant, but they jumped up and down on the stained mattress like grasshoppers. "This calls for a special meal," Mamá said. That evening she went out and bought enchiladas, rice, and beans.

After supper, Papá lay on the bed to rest his back. "I've been thinking about where we go from here," he said, lighting up a cigarette. *Back to Santa Maria, of course. Where else?* I thought. Papá bit his lower lip and continued. "It's the rainy season; there's little work in the fields during this time, and my back is getting worse." He paused, puffed on his cigarette, and went on, "The only sure thing is Roberto's janitorial job. What if he goes back to Santa Maria and the rest of us go to Guadalajara and stay with my sister Chana? It'll give me a chance to see a *curandera* about my back. In the spring, when I am cured, we can go back to Santa Maria and I can work in the fields again." My heart fell to my stomach. I did not want to miss more school. I wanted to tell Papá that I did not like his idea, but I did not say anything. Papá never allowed us to disagree with him. He said it was disrespectful.

"What if Panchito goes back with Roberto?" Mamá said. "That way he can help him at work and both can attend school." I knew Mamá had read my mind. She winked at me when she saw me smile.

"You're a grown man, a real *macho*," Papá said, directing his attention to my brother. "You can take care of Panchito. *Verdad, mijo*." My brother grinned and nodded.

The thought of being apart from Papá, Mamá, and my brothers and sister saddened me, but the idea of missing school and not being with Roberto pained me even more.

"I'll go back with him, but I'll miss you," I said, holding back my tears.

"We'll miss you too," Mamá said, wiping her eyes.

"I'll send you money every month when I get paid," Roberto said proudly.

"You're a good son," Papá said, motioning for Roberto to sit by his side on the bed.

"They're all a blessing," Mamá added, smiling at Roberto and me and hugging Rorra, Torito, and Trampita.

We decided to leave the hotel that evening to avoid paying for another night. I went with Mamá to the office to check out. I wanted to look at the rocks one more time. The clerk caught my eye and said, "Those are copper pyrite rocks."

"They look like gold," I replied.

"It's fool's gold." He picked up the rock I had taken before and handed it to me. "Here, you can have this one. It'll bring you good luck."

I glanced at Mamá. She smiled and nodded. "Thanks," I said, taking the rock and placing it in my pocket. *I am glad I returned it and didn't throw it away,* I thought.

We finished packing and headed to the bus station on foot. It was starting to rain, so we hurried. Roberto, Papá, Trampita, and I carried the cardboard boxes. Mamá held Rorra by the hand. Torito and Rubén ran behind us, trying to keep up. "Not so fast!" they cried out. "Wait for us!" Armed guards stopped us at the border gate and asked us for documentation. Their green uniforms gave me the chills. Papá showed them our papers, and they let us cross to Nogales, Arizona.

We were dripping wet by the time we arrived at the bus station. Mamá went up to the counter and bought two one-way tickets to Santa Maria for Roberto and me and five tickets to Guadalajara for the rest of the family. We went to the restroom and dried ourselves with paper towels, then sat in silence on a wooden bench, waiting for the bus. Torito and Trampita were fidgety. They jumped off the bench, ran to the pinball machine, and pushed each other, trying to pull on the handle. Papá made a sharp hissing sound like a rattlesnake to get their attention. He made this noise whenever he was annoyed with something we were doing. They did not hear him, so he hissed louder, but the loudspeaker announcing departures and arrivals drowned it out. With a slight tilt of his head toward the pinball machine, Papá motioned for me to get Trampita and Torito. Papá gave them a stern look and told them to sit and be quiet. I sat between Trampita and Torito and placed my arms around them. I felt sad, thinking how much I was going to miss them.

I glanced at the clock on the wall and went outside to get fresh air. It was pouring rain. Looking up at the dark sky, I wished we were all going back to Santa Maria together. I heard an announcement over the loudspeaker, but I did not pay attention. "Our bus is here, Panchito," Roberto said, as he and the rest of my family approached me from behind. Roberto and I hugged Papá and Mamá and kissed our brothers and sister.

"Que Dios los bendiga," Mamá said, giving us her blessing. Tears came to her eyes as she forced a smile. Roberto and I climbed onto the bus. We took our seat, wiped the fog off the window, and waved. The rain pelted the bus with full force as it pulled away.

Across the aisle, a little boy played horse on his father's lap. He jumped up and down and repeatedly smacked the side of his legs, shouting, "Faster, faster!" I turned away, closed my eyes, and leaned on Roberto's shoulder. I wept silently until I fell asleep.

When I woke up, the rain had disappeared. A strong wind whipped up dust, debris, and gravel and forced the bus to slow down to a snail's pace. Once the wind died down, the bus pulled over at a rest stop next to an old gas station and market. Roberto and I climbed down to stretch our legs. On the side of the station was a make-shift open stand braced by four posts. Hanging from one of the upper-right posts was a crate with a wooden crucifix on it. Roberto and I made the sign of the cross and bowed our heads. I prayed silently that my family would arrive safely in Guadalajara. We climbed back on the bus and continued our journey.

We finally arrived in Santa Maria in the early evening of the next day. We took a cab to Bonetti Ranch, where we were welcomed by a torrential downpour and a pack of bony stray dogs. The cab drove slowly, bumping up and down and swaying from side to side as it hit potholes full of water. It felt as though we were in a ship in the middle of a stormy sea. Our barrack was cold and lifeless. We placed our boxes on the floor and turned on the kitchen light. "Well, here we are, Panchito," Roberto said sadly. When he saw me choke up, he added, "Time will go by fast, you'll see."

"Not fast enough," I said. We unpacked our boxes and went to bed. Neither one of us slept well that night.

Home Alone

The next morning Roberto and I woke up to the rattling sound of the alarm clock. I turned it off and listened to the silence of dawn. The sounds of Papá's coughing, the rattle of his aspirin bottle, and the rolling of Mamá's twelve-inch lead pipe as she pressed dough to make tortillas were absent. So too were the smells of *chorizo* and scrambled eggs. I missed Mamá's gentle tapping on my shoulders and tugging of the blanket to wake me up. In the distance I heard the barking of dogs. Every morning they circled the large, empty oil barrels that served as garbage cans. As I got dressed, I heard farm workers warming their car engines before leaving to look for work picking carrots or thinning lettuce.

What I did not miss that morning was emptying the bedpan, which had been one of my regular chores. Papá, Mamá, and my younger brothers and sister used it, but

Roberto and I did not. I hated taking out the Folgers coffee can and emptying it in the outhouse every morning before I went to school. I felt embarrassed to be seen by our neighbors, especially the girls. Every day, I tried to convince Mamá that one of my younger brothers, Trampita or Torito, should take over that task, but she did not agree. Holding the bedpan behind me, I would poke my head out the front door to make sure the coast was clear. I would rush to the outhouse, holding the bedpan steady and trying to chase away a pack of hungry dogs that followed me. Don Pancho, one of our neighbors, knew how much I disliked emptying the bedpan and teased me whenever I ran into him. One morning he was coming out of the outhouse as I carried the Folgers coffee can. "What do you have there, Panchito?" he said, smirking.

"Your coffee and *pan dulce*," I shot back angrily. He was taken by surprise as much as I was. He told Papá, who scolded me for being disrespectful. But Don Pancho never made fun of me again.

Alone in the barrack, Roberto and I took care of regular chores. We made our bed, swept and mopped the floor, and fixed breakfast. My brother washed the dishes and I dried them and put them away. We left the house sparkling clean, just as we did every morning before heading off for school.

Roberto dropped me off at El Camino Junior High School on his way to Santa Maria High School. I was excited to be back at school, but nervous. How far behind in my classes would I be? What would my teachers and classmates say to me? My teachers, Mr. Ken Milo and Miss Ehlis, must have known how I felt because they did not ask me any questions. They seemed happy to see me back. My classmates acted as if I had never left. I figured my teachers must have said something about it to them or they simply forgot. I felt lucky, but anxious, expecting one of them to ask or to say something at any moment. No one asked, but in case they did, I had an answer. I would tell them that the Border Patrol officer had made a mistake thinking I was here illegally, that once I proved to him I was born in Colton, California, he let me back in.

Roberto was late picking me up from school that afternoon. I knew something was wrong as soon as I saw him. He looked troubled.

"I lost my job at Main Street School," he said, teary-eyed.

"What do you mean?" I asked in a panic.

"Mr. Sims was angry with me because I missed so many weeks from work. He said he didn't know where I was, so he hired someone else."

"Didn't you tell him what happened?" I asked.

"Of course not!" he snapped. "I couldn't tell him. When I got the job I said I was an American citizen." He rested his head on the steering wheel, gripping it with both hands. His knuckles turned white. "This means we'll have to go back to the fields." My heart fell to my stomach.

"Again!" I exclaimed, clenching my teeth. My shoulders felt heavier than ever.

For the next two weeks, Roberto and I worked picking carrots and thinning lettuce after school and on weekends when it did not rain. We thinned lettuce using a short hoe. When our backs hurt from stooping over, we thinned on our knees. To ease the pain, we took turns lying flat on our stomachs in the furrows and pressing down on each other's backs with our hands. Working together all day, Saturday and Sunday, Roberto and I managed to finish an acre, for which we were paid sixteen dollars.

Picking carrots was easier than thinning lettuce, but a lot messier. The ground was usually muddy, so our shoes and pants got soaked in mud. We worked on our knees, pulling the carrots out of the ground after they were loosened by a tractor-plow. We topped off the leaves by hand and dumped the carrots in a bucket until it was full. We then emptied the bucket into a burlap sack. We got paid fifteen cents a sack.

During that time we never had carrots or lettuce with our meals. Since neither of us knew how to cook, baloney sandwiches replaced Mamá's delicious *taquitos*. At suppertime, the hand can opener quickly became our best friend. Almost every day we ate canned ravioli with either canned peas or canned corn. Other times we had chicken noodle soup. For dessert we had a peanut butter and jam sand-wich or vanilla ice cream. For breakfast we had scrambled eggs or Cream of Wheat with globs of butter and sugar.

Roberto gave up eating baloney sandwiches when he got a part-time job working at noon at Velva's Freeze, a hamburger and ice cream store located on Broadway, a few blocks from the high school. During the lunch hour on school days, he walked to Velva's Freeze and helped serve ice cream cones. He got paid a dollar an hour and had a hamburger with french fries and a Coke every day.

Mary O'Neill, the owner of Velva's Freeze, was a child-less widow in her late fifties. She was short and thin. Her wrinkly, pale skin blended with her short gray hair, and her dark blue eyes sparkled when she talked. Everything she wore was white, including her shoes. The only colors on her were the ketchup and mustard stains on her apron. She liked my brother, and when she found out that he and I were living alone, she invited us to dinner on Saturday. We were to meet her at five-thirty at the ice cream store.

That Saturday afternoon Roberto and I stopped picking carrots at four o'clock and went home to get ready. We were excited and a bit anxious about eating in a restau-rant for the first time. I tried to imagine what it would be like. We heated water in a large pot and poured it into a large aluminum tub. We took a bath in the shed, which was attached to the side of our barrack. Papá built it with discarded wood from the city dump. We used Fab laundry detergent to wash our hair because soap and shampoo were too mild to cut the sulfur and oil in the water. We dressed in our best clothes and arrived at Velva's Freeze on time.

"I am so glad you're joining me," Mary said. "Have you been to the Far Western in Guadalupe?"

"We've been to Guadalupe, but not the Far Western," Roberto responded.

"Good! We'll go there," she said enthusiastically. "They're famous for their steaks."

A steak dinner sounded a lot better than canned ravioli. The Far Western restaurant was about nine miles from downtown Santa Maria. It was dimly lit and had dark brown wooden tables and chairs that were thick and heavy. In the middle of one of the dark-paneled walls hung a stuffed moose head with long antlers. I heard deep voices and the clinking of glasses coming from another room. "It's the bar," Mary said, noticing how I was craning to see what it was. "You can't go there—you're too young." She chuckled and lit a cigarette. The waiter, dressed as a cowboy, brought us the menu. I glanced through it, noticing the high prices and a long list of different kinds of steak. I always thought steak was steak.

"What kind of steak do you like?" Mary asked, putting down her menu. Roberto had a blank look on his face. She waited for an answer. I hated her patience at that moment. I expected her to tell us. At home we had no choices; we ate whatever Mamá cooked.

Breaking the long silence, I finally said: "I'll have whatever you have."

"I am going to have New York steak," she answered.

"Me too," I said quickly.

"Good. What about you, Roberto?"

My brother's face turned red. He glanced at me from the corner of his eye, brought the menu up to his face, and said: "I'll have the same."

"And to drink?" she asked.

"Just water, please," Roberto answered.

"Me too," I said.

"Well, I am going to have a glass of red wine. It goes well with steak," she said. I did not quite understand why red wine and steak went together. Then I noticed that Mary placed one hand on her lap and the other on the table. Papá and Mamá taught us to always have both hands on the table. Roberto must have noticed it too, because he kept changing his mind. One minute he would have both hands on the table, the next minute only one. He finally settled on one, just like Mary. I figured it was the right thing to do, so I did the same. The next thing that caught my attention was that Mary's napkin had disappeared. Roberto's napkin and mine were still on the table. At home we did not have napkins. After taking a sip of wine, Mary lifted her napkin and wiped the corners of her mouth, and then her napkin again disappeared underneath the table. I thought she had dropped it. I pretended to drop mine. As I leaned down to pick it up, I saw Mary's napkin was on her lap. I placed mine on my lap and kicked Roberto under the table at the same time so that he would notice. He caught my signal and placed his napkin on his lap too. During the rest of the meal, Roberto and I did exactly what Mary did. I figured she must have noticed what we were doing because she did things very slowly, giving us time to follow. Roberto and I did not enjoy our meal, but we had a good time being with Mary.

Roberto and I continued going to school and working in the fields after school and on weekends. We missed our family and worried about not being able to send them money to help them out. We were barely making ends meet ourselves. But things were about to change.

One day after school, Roberto came to pick me up at El Camino Junior High as usual. I heard the screeching of tires as he turned the corner and came to a halt. *Something must be wrong,* I thought. *Why is he in such a hurry? I hope it's not bad news from Mexico.* When I saw him beaming, his two large front teeth more visible than ever, I was relieved. "Guess what, Panchito?" he said, out of breath. Before I had a chance to ask, he blurted out, "I got my job back! I'll start Monday."

"At Main Street School?"

"Yes! Mr. Sims offered me the job back. He told me that the man who replaced me didn't work out. He was fired. I feel bad for him, but it's great for us, Panchito. It's my ticket out of the fields and to more money."

I was happy, but sad too. It meant that I would have to work in the fields after school by myself. My brother noticed my excitement disappear. "You can help me like before," he said, putting his arm around me. "And, who knows, maybe I can get you a job there too. Come on, cheer up!" That evening we celebrated with extra helpings of ravioli and vanilla ice cream.

We picked carrots that weekend. All day Sunday at work I could hardly wait for the day to end. I savored the thought of helping Roberto clean Main Street School and not having to work in the fields any longer after school. I glanced over at Roberto, who was emptying his bucket into a sack. He towered above the long row of full sacks lined up behind him. The gray clouds sailed above us, breaking up into smaller ones, leaving little openings of blue sky.

Starting that following Monday, Roberto and I spent more time at school and work than at home. Roberto picked me up after school, and we drove directly to Main Street School to clean it. We headed down to the basement of the main building to the janitor's room to get the cleaning cart. Roberto had keys to every room and building. He carried them on a key chain attached to the side of his belt. The keys clanged as he walked, and the more noise they made, the more he stuck out his chest and lifted his chin. We worked like clockwork. While Roberto cleared off and dusted the tables, I emptied the trash. Then I placed the chairs on the tables to clear the floor for him to sweep with a dust mop. After he swept, he placed the chairs back in their place while I cleaned the black-boards. We cleaned the boys' and girls' bathrooms last. At nine o'clock we went home, ate dinner, finished our homework, and went to bed. On Saturdays and Sundays we continued working in the fields, picking carrots and thinning lettuce.

At the end of every two weeks, Roberto got a check from the Santa Maria school district, which he cashed to buy groceries and other necessities. Any leftover money he hid underneath our mattress and later sent to our family in Mexico in care of our *tía* Chana, Papá's older sister, with whom our family was staying in Tlaquepaque, a suburb of Guadalajara.

One evening when we got home after work, we discovered that someone had broken in our house and stolen our cash. That month we could not send money to our parents. From that day on, Roberto hid the cash inside a chipped ceramic bust of Jesus Christ that we had found in the public dump.

Stepping Out

Every time Roberto and I went home in the evenings to an empty house, I felt lonely. Sometimes I imagined hearing the laughter and bickering of my brothers and sister. I longed for the smell and taste of home cooking, especially flour tortillas, *frijoles de la olla*, and *carne con chile*. I missed seeing Papá's eyes water when he listened to Mexican music on the radio and hearing him repeat stories about Mexico when he was young. I even missed his bad moods and his constant complaints about his back pain and headaches. I buried my head in my schoolbooks. I wanted to keep on learning and to escape the loneliness I felt for my family.

At school I felt alone most of the time, but I did get some attention from my classmates because I did well in math. Mr. Milo arranged our desks according to how well we did on math tests. The student with the highest score had the honor of sitting in the front seat, first row. A few times I took the first seat, but most of the time I sat in the second one. Marjorie Ito, the daughter of the Japanese sharecropper for whom we picked strawberries, almost always took first place. My classmates called me "hotshot" and teased me because I worked hard. I did not mind it. I knew they were being friendly. Besides, I wanted to be accepted and, most of all, respected. Papá insisted on our being respectful and respected. "If you respect others, they will respect you," he often said.

To make friends, I began to pay close attention to what my classmates did and talked about. During recess, the girls talked about boys, music, and dancing. The boys discussed sports, cars, and girls. When they got together, they talked about different songs and singers and about going to dances on Saturday nights at the Veterans Memorial Building, which was across the street from El Camino Junior High. Sometimes their animated conversations turned into arguments about the best singer or song. Many of the song titles were funny: "Jailhouse Rock," "Rock Around the Clock," and "Venus in Blue Jeans." I tried to make sense out of them and pictured them in my mind. Why would a rock circle a clock? Why would the planet Venus dress in jeans? I soon discovered that rock 'n' roll was a type of popular music. For me, music and dancing were more interesting and fun than sports or cars.

Roberto and I began to tune in to rock 'n' roll music on the radio. We listened to Little Richard and Elvis Presley. I enjoyed the rhythm, but I did not pay much attention to the words like I did with Mexican music. Of all the popular singers, I liked Elvis the best. His fast songs released energy in my legs and made them move almost on their own. His slow songs were melancholy, like some Mexican ranchera songs.

Listening to Elvis paid off. During rainy days, when we could not go outside for recess, we stayed in our homeroom and played games. Miss Ehlis, our homeroom teacher, suggested forming small groups and coming up with skits for the whole class. I came up with the idea of creating a skit to show how banks charged interest on loans, since we were studying how to figure percentages in Mr. Milo's math class. Everyone in my group made a face. "What about something with music?" one of them said enthusiastically.

"Yeah, rock 'n' roll," another responded.

Here is my chance, I thought. "How about me doing one of Elvis's songs?" I said nervously. They all dropped their jaws and looked at me as though they had seen a ghost.

"You! Doing Elvis? Elvis with a Mexican accent!" one said, laughing. Others snickered.

I felt blood rushing to my face. I clenched my hands and, like a bullfighter facing the bull, I demanded, "Why not?" They all laughed. "Why not?" I repeated, annoyed. Their laughter died out.

"You're dead serious, aren't you? Okay, let's go for it!" exclaimed Robert Lindsay, an Elvis fan.

Next day Robert Lindsay brought in several of Elvis's records and played parts of them. I don't recall exactly why, but I picked "Treat Me Like a Fool." I took the record home and played it over and over on a record player that Roberto borrowed from Main Street School. I wrote the lyrics down and memorized them. The next time it rained during recess, it would be our group's turn to perform. That night I prayed for sunshine, but my prayers were not answered. It poured the next morning. I felt butterflies in my stomach. The idea of staying home went through my mind several times, but I had no choice. I had to do it.

At recess, my group was ready. They were my backup singers and moral support. Robert Lindsay introduced me as Elvis, and the class burst out laughing. Miss Ehlis stood in the back of the room with her arms crossed, smiling. My hands were cold and clammy. The record started and I began to lip-synch the longest song of my life. "Treat me like a fool. Treat me mean and cruel, but love me..." Everyone shouted and clapped, drowning out the music. Robert Lindsay raised the volume, and the class raised their own volume. Finally Miss Ehlis told everyone to quiet down. She asked me to start over. I felt more at ease and began the song again. My group swayed and clapped to the rhythm of the song. When it was over, everyone cheered and clapped, including Miss Ehlis. Some yelled out, "That was cool, Frankie!" From that day on, I was an Elvis fan.

I told Roberto about my performance and asked him if we could attend the dance at the Veterans Memorial on Saturday night.

"You don't know how to dance and neither do I," he said.

"We can watch and listen to the music. Everyone talks about the dances at the Vets. They even announce them on the radio."

"They talk about the dances at my school too, but they say guys get drunk and get into fights."

"We can always leave if that happens. Come on, just once," I insisted. Roberto finally gave in. It was the first time we had gone out for fun by ourselves. We had gone to see Mexican movies in Fresno on rainy days when it was too wet to pick cotton, but it was always with our parents.

We arrived at the Veterans Memorial an hour after the dance started. Roberto parked the car in front of El Camino Junior High, right across the street from a circular lit park, next to the Vets building. Groups of boys were scattered throughout the park and in front of the building. Small clouds of cigarette smoke came up from the middle of their huddles. Roberto and I stayed in the car, listening to the radio and watching like two investigators. Strings of boys and girls walked in and out the building, talking, laughing, and swaying to the music that blasted through the entrance door.

We finally got the courage to get out of the car. We cut our way through the crowd, bumping shoulders with boys who were standing in the doorway eyeing the girls passing by. We paid for our tickets and walked in. The music blared and vibrated throughout the building, which was set up like a theater. It had rows of seats on either side, a stage at the front, and an open space in the middle for dancing. The dim lights made it hard to see faces from across the room. The band onstage announced the next song and began to play it. Some of the songs I recognized because I had heard them on the radio, but many of them were new to me. The titles, "Bird Dog," "See You Later, Alligator," "Great Balls of Fire," amused me. Few people danced. Most of the boys stood on one side of the dance floor and the girls on the other side. *Maybe they don't know how to dance either*, I thought.

Roberto and I fit in perfectly. I listened to the music, not paying much attention to the lyrics, and studied the few couples dancing. Roberto seemed distracted, so I leaned over and whispered loudly in his ear to pay attention to the dancers. "Why?" he yelled back, annoyed. I did not think he would appreciate my telling him the reason right there and then.

"I'll tell you later."

We left the dance having spent not an ounce of energy on the dance floor, but many of the dance moves were etched in my mind. That night when we returned home, I had ringing in my ears and my clothes smelled like the ashtray in the principal's office at Main Street School. I turned on the radio and tuned it to the station that played rock 'n' roll music. "Haven't you had enough?" Roberto asked, looking puzzled. After a few commercial announcements, "Rock Around the Clock" by Bill Haley and the Comets came on. I grabbed Roberto's hands and started dancing, trying to imitate some of the moves I had witnessed at the Vets. *"Te has vuelto loco!"* he cried out, quickly pulling back his hands.

"I am not crazy! Come on, Roberto, let's dance!"

"Guys don't dance with each other," he said, laughing. "Besides, we don't know how."

"But if we don't try, we'll never learn. Come on," I insisted. "Remember at the Vets. Some of the girls danced with each other. Why? Because guys didn't ask them."

"Maybe the guys didn't know how."

"That's my point," I said. "If we learn..."

"I see your point, Panchito. We'll meet girls and make new friends."

"Ándale," I said in agreement. "And have lots of fun too."

From that moment on, Roberto and I were secret dance

partners. We practiced about half an hour every day, after our ravioli dinners. We rarely missed going to the Vets on Saturday nights and eventually worked up the courage to ask girls to dance. My brother called me *Resortes*, "Rubber Legs."

I made friends with several classmates who attended the Vets regularly. Peggy Dossen was one of them. We always danced the last song. She was in my homeroom class and often teased me about having imitated Elvis. Whenever she did, I would say, "Treat me like a fool. Treat me mean and cruel, but love me." She would laugh as though it was the first time she had heard me say it.

One Friday after school, Peggy said she was not sure she could attend the next Vets dance. She asked me to call her Saturday night before Roberto and I left for the dance. She wrote her telephone number on a piece of paper from her binder, handed it to me, and ran to catch her ride before I had a chance to say anything. We did not have a telephone at home. I had never used one. My mind raced a mile a minute as I tried to figure out what to do. Then Joe and Espy Martínez's names popped into my mind. They were our neighbors with whom we shared the outhouse and garbage cans and the only ones at the ranch who had a phone. I decided to ask them if I could use it.

I nervously walked over to their barrack, followed by a pack of barking dogs. Joe greeted me and invited me in.

"Would you mind if I used your phone?" I asked.

"Of course not, Panchito, " Espy said. "Go right ahead. It's on the table." The black phone was just like the phone in the principal's office. I took out the piece of notepaper with Peggy's number from my shirt pocket, unfolded it, and placed it next to the phone. I did not know what to do next. I glanced over at Espy, who caught my eye. "What's the matter, Panchito? Did you forget the number?"

"No," I responded, hesitating. She must have noticed the plea for help in my eyes.

"Here, let me dial it for you," she said, picking up the receiver. As I read out the numbers, she dialed them, one by one, slowly, giving me a chance to see how she did it. She then placed the receiver in my left hand, and I lifted it to my ear. I felt the sweat in the palm of my hand. After the third ring, I heard, "Hello." I recognized Peggy's voice. "Hello," she repeated, "is anybody there?"

"Peggy, it's me," I said in a whisper.

"Speak louder," she said. "I can hardly hear you." I looked over at Joe and Espy, who pretended not to pay attention.

"It's me, Francisco," I responded, raising my voice.

"I can't make the dance tonight. Sorry. I have to baby-sit. Are you going?"

"I think so." I was disappointed but anxious to end the conversation. I did not like talking to Peggy on the phone because I could not see her face. My answers to her questions were brief, followed by dead silence. I figured she got tired of trying to get me to talk.

"I've got to go. See you at school," she said sharply.

"Yes," I said, easing my tight grip on the receiver. I hung up. The receiver was moist. I wiped it off on my shirtsleeve, thanked Joe and Espy, and darted out before they had a chance to ask me any questions.

The next time I saw Peggy, she asked me to walk her home after school. When Roberto came to pick me up, I told him that I would meet him at work and explained why. Peggy's house was a few blocks from Main Street School, on the east side of town. The houses in Peggy's neighborhood were different from the barracks in Bonetti Ranch. They had sidewalks, front lawns, and beautiful flower gardens. I did not have to watch out for potholes or stray dogs. I had been in a house once before. I was in the fifth grade when my friend Carl invited me to his home to see his coin collection. Peggy's house was twice as big as Carl's house. It was a two-story home with a double garage.

We were greeted at the door by a small white poodle with a red silk ribbon tied to its tail. "This is Skippy," Peggy said. She picked him up, gave him a light kiss, and set him back down on the soft, white rug. The air had a sweet, perfume smell. As we passed by the kitchen, I noticed it had no odor at all. I thought this was odd. Our kitchen always had a smell. Peggy introduced me to her parents, who were sitting in a spacious living room. "Mom and Dad, this is Francisco Jiménez, a friend of mine. The teachers and some kids call him Frankie." I felt butterflies in my stomach.

"Glad to meet you," I said, wiping my sweaty hand on the side of my pants before shaking hands with Peggy's father.

"Likewise, Frankie," he said, gripping my hand and shaking it several times. His voice was deep and strong like Papá's.

"Are you Spanish?" Mrs. Dossen asked politely. "I detect a strong accent."

"I am Mexican," I said proudly. "But born in Colton, California," I quickly added.

"That's interesting," Mr. Dossen said after a short silence. His wife nodded her head and smiled uneasily.

"Come on, Frankie, I'll show you my room," Peggy said, grabbing my hand. I pulled it away as I glanced at her parents, who seemed upset. Peggy and I climbed the stairs. Her poodle led the way, wagging its tail. Her room was as large as our kitchen and bedroom combined. It had wall-to-wall white carpeting. The pink lace curtains in the two large windows matched the color of her bedspread, which was thick and fluffy. Her closet, full of clothes, was built into the wall, and the top of her dresser was covered with small perfume bottles, lipsticks, and miniature dolls.

The outside frame of the mirror on the dresser was full of pictures of her family and her poodle.

"It's nice!" I exclaimed.

"I am glad you like it." She removed several large stuffed animals from the bed and sat on the edge of it. "Here, sit next to me," she said.

I felt uncomfortable being alone with her in the room. *Papá and Mamá would never allow this*, I thought. It was disrespectful, especially to her parents. "I'd better get going," I said. "It's getting late."

"Late for what?" she said, laughing. She grabbed my arm and pulled me toward her, trying to force me to sit next to her. I dug my heels in the thick carpet and leaned backward. "What's wrong with you?" she said, annoyed. The dog sensed Peggy was upset and started barking at me and pulling at my pant leg.

"Peggy, what's wrong with Skippy?" her mother cried out from downstairs. "You'd better come down right now!"

Peggy quieted the dog, picked him up, and, without saying a word to me, carried him downstairs. I gladly followed them. I said good-bye to her parents and headed for the door. "Thanks for walking me home," Peggy said.

"You're welcome," I said. "See you at school."

"Sure," she responded. "See ya."

The next day when I saw Peggy at school, she avoided me, even outside of class. She did not walk home after school. When I saw her mother waiting in the car, I waved

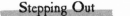

to her, but she looked the other way. I could not under-stand why. The following day I cornered Peggy in the hallway and asked her why she was avoiding me. She walked away and refused to talk to me. I was hurt and puzzled.

Roberto and I continued going to the dances at the Vets, but they were not fun anymore. Peggy had stopped going, and more and more boys began drinking and picking fights. We were afraid of getting in trouble, so we stopped attending as often as before. We did not stop lis-tening to music, however. At home we danced with each other or with the mop or broom to keep in shape. Instead of the Vets, we sometimes went to the movie theater. Watching American movies was different for Roberto and me. We did not go to American movies before because Papá did not understand English. Sometimes on rainy days when we did not work, our family went to watch Mexican cowboy movies. They were Papá's favorite. They reminded him of his childhood and living in the country-side, where horses were the only means of transportation. I enjoyed American movies because they helped me im-prove my English and gave me something to talk about with my classmates.

Together Again

We knew our family would return from Mexico sometime in early April, but we did not know exactly what day. In the evenings we rushed home after work, hoping to see them. Each time we found an empty house we were disappointed, but hopeful and excited that the next day would be it. We wanted to surprise them when they came home, so we frequented the public dump on early Saturday evenings to look for discarded paint and linoleum to brighten the inside of our house. We painted the kitchen and replaced the worn-out linoleum with new pieces of different colors and shapes, making the floor look like a quilt. In his wood-shop class, Roberto made a cupboard with a planter on top and filled it with plastic flowers. He placed it against the end of the kitchen sink, dividing the kitchen and dining area. Before going to school every morning, we made sure that the house was perfectly clean.

The long-awaited day finally arrived. It was early Sunday evening. Roberto and I were doing our homework at the kitchen table when we heard the dogs barking. We jumped up and ran out the door. A yellow cab came around the corner and parked in front. All four doors of the cab flew open like the petals of a flower. I went around the front of the car to the other side, where Papá and Mamá stood with open arms. I felt like a child running to them. I did not know whom to hug first. Papá gave me a kiss on the forehead, the first kiss he had ever given me. Trampita, Rorra, and Torito jumped up and down and ran around Papá, Mamá, Roberto, and me, in a circle, laughing hysterically, touching our legs and bumping into one another. The cab driver stood leaning against the rear bumper, waiting for Papá to pay him. Roberto and I unloaded the cardboard boxes from the trunk and ran into the house, anxious to show Papá and Mamá what we had done.

"It's beautiful, *mijo!*" Mamá said, looking all around at the brightly painted kitchen, the colorful floor, and the cupboard with plastic flowers.

"This must have been expensive," Papá said, running his hands across the wood.

"I didn't buy it. I made it at school," Roberto responded proudly.

"So they teach you this at school? That's good, *mijo*. Maybe you'll be a carpenter."

"Like Saint Joseph," Mamá said. "I'd like that."

"Tell us about Mexico," Roberto said, trying to draw the attention away from himself.

"We will in a minute," Mamá answered, "but first, we have a surprise for you." She kneeled and opened one of the cardboard boxes and pulled out a small statue of the *Santo Niño de Atocha*. "This is for you, Roberto."

My brother was awed and speechless. He grabbed the statue firmly with both hands, making sure not to drop it. He examined it from top to bottom and side to side.

"Thank you, Mamá," he said, teary-eyed.

"He cured you when you were sick," Roberto said, turning to Torito and handing him the statue.

"I know," Torito said, reaching out to hold it.

"It was a miracle," I said, remembering how Mamá had made Torito an outfit just like the one the Holy Child Jesus wore in a picture prayer card Papá carried in his wallet. We all prayed to the *Santo Niño* until my brother got well.

"And for you, Panchito, we got you this new bust of Jesus Christ to replace the one that's chipped," she said. "It's smaller, but nicer."

I took it carefully and gave Mamá a hug. The ceramic piece was the suffering face of Christ wearing a crown of thorns made from sharp nails. Blood dripped from his forehead and his sad eyes looked upward in prayer. It made me feel sad.

After we told them about school and work, Papá began to tell us about their stay in Mexico. "We had some ups and downs," Papá said, lighting up a Camel cigarette. "It was hard on your *tía* Chana. She and her family don't have much, but they made us feel at home. With the money you sent us, we helped out with groceries, but it was rough at times."

"If it hadn't been for you boys, I don't know what we would have done," Mamá said. She sighed and continued. "But the kids had a good time, except for Trampita..."

"I was hit by a bus," Trampita blurted out.

"He wasn't paying attention," Papá said, giving him a stern look for interrupting. "He was playing ball with his cousins out in the street. Luckily, he was not seriously hurt, but it scared us." Trampita grinned and shrugged his shoulders sheepishly.

"Papá has some more good news!" Mamá said excitedly. "Remember how Papá suffered from back pain? Well, you tell them, *viejo*."

Papá chuckled and stood up straight. "See, my back is much better." He sat down and continued. "I am cured. A *curandera* took care of me. She discovered I had been hexed."

"Really?" I said, recalling Doña María, a *curandera* in Tent City who tried to cure Torito when he was sick.

There was something about her that made me nervous.

"How did she find out?" Roberto asked.

"I went to her hut in the outskirts of Tlaquepaque. It was like the garage we lived in in Selma. It had a dirt floor and no electricity. Behind it was a corral where she raised chickens and pigs. In one corner of the hut was a small table covered in black cloth. In the opposite corner was an altar with the *Virgen de Guadalupe*. It was surrounded with small, lit candles, pieces of clothing, wreaths, dried flowers, burning incense, and holy cards. We sat at the table facing each other and drank bitter tea that made me sleepy. She then had me strip to my waist and lie facedown on a straw mat. She massaged my back with raw eggs and chanted in Huichol. I understood one or two words because your grandmother used to speak it. I fell into a deep sleep. When I woke up, I was soaked in sweat and my face was in the middle of a thick pool of blood, covered with mucus. It had a foul smell, like dead flesh. She told me I had vomited it during my sleep."

"Maybe she put it there while you were asleep," I said.

"Sounds like you don't believe me, *mijo*, but it's true." Papá sounded annoyed.

"I bet the devil had something to do with it," Roberto said. "When you were very sick in Corcoran, Papá, I saw the devil in the glass of water you kept next to your bed."

"I thought the glass of water was to keep evil spirits away," I said.

"You don't believe I saw the devil?" Roberto said, raising his voice and making a face at me.

"I am not sure," I answered hesitantly. "Maybe you imagined it. Besides, how do we know he really exists?"

"You'd better believe, or else..."

"Don't say it," Mamá interrupted. "The point is Papá is feeling better, and we should thank God for it."

We continued late into the night, catching up on all the things we had done during the time we were apart. That night, before I went to bed, I prayed and thanked God our family was back together again. I placed the bust of Jesus Christ underneath my pillow and fell asleep.

Back to the Fields

I was happy to be with my family again, but unhappy that I had to return to the fields. Now that Papá felt better, he started working for Ito again. I did too. I took the bus home after school and joined Papá picking strawberries. I got paid for picking, but not for helping my brother clean Main Street School.

I missed being with Roberto. While I worked, I daydreamed about going to the Vets dances and played rock 'n' roll tunes in my head. Most of the time, I studied things I needed to learn for school. I wrote the information in a small notepad, which I carried in my shirt pocket, and memorized it while I picked.

Weekends were special. Roberto joined Papá and me in the fields, and, during our half-hour lunch break, Roberto and I listened to Papá and the *braceros* tell stories about Mexico. One time Papá told us how he had joined the

Cristero Revolt in 1926, when he was sixteen, and had been wounded in the knee and thrown in jail for six months. "See the scar?" he said with pride, pulling up his left pant leg. "The bullet is still there. Feel it." I placed my finger on the jagged mark. "Put pressure on it, *mijo*." I felt a hard piece of lead, the size of a marble, swim inside Papá's knee as he rotated his leg. "Those were tough times," he went on. "You could smell death in the air. The fields were irrigated with blood and men hung from trees like rotting fruit." After he finished telling the story, he turned on the car radio to listen to Mexican music. I changed the channel to rock 'n' roll, and Papá got upset. He said it was junk and changed it back.

Papá often talked about becoming a strawberry sharecropper and not having to work for someone else. So when Papá found out that a rancher was looking for sharecroppers, he felt torn. He felt a certain loyalty to Ito because he had sponsored us when we applied for our visas. He knew that without Ito's help, we could not have come back legally as quickly as we did. He went back and forth, trying to decide what to do. Joe García, one of our neighbors, who had served in World War II, insisted that Papá form a partnership with him, taking care of six acres, three acres each, of newly planted strawberries in a parcel of land located between Santa Maria and Guadalupe. Papá was finally convinced. He decided to continue working for Ito six days a week, except Sundays, and to be a sharecropper.

Sharecropping was not easy. The rancher provided the land and plants, but the sharecroppers were responsible for everything else. We had the hands to work the land, but not the equipment. Papá and Joe García borrowed money from a savings and loan company to buy a small tractor, tools, wood to build a shed to store them, and an outhouse. Papá also bought on credit a 1953 Buick to replace the *Carcachita*. Roberto drove the Buick to school and work. Papá and Mamá drove an old DeSoto that Mr. Donovan, a rancher, had given them in exchange for some work Papá had done for him.

The three acres consumed all our resources and time. Papá worked for Ito from seven in the morning until five-thirty in the afternoon. He would come home, have a quick supper, and head out with Trampita and me to our three acres, where we worked until dusk. Papá tilled the soil with the tractor while Trampita and I pulled out weeds. We dug them out with a hand shovel, making sure not to damage the delicate plants. At times the ground was so hard that we had to dig the shovel into the ground with both hands, pushing in with the weight of our bodies. There were hundreds of *coquitos*, weeds that had a small brown nut at the end of their roots. We had to dig out the nut, otherwise the weed would sprout again. Some patches were so dense with weeds that strawberry plants struggled to survive.

Once we cleared the weeds, we broke mud clods with

short hoes and shovels. At times it seemed like a losing battle. Every time Papá tilled the furrows, more mud clods bubbled up, leaving the ground coarse and uneven again. We pounded the furrows with shovel blades and hoes, trying to break down the soil. The ground was as stubborn as the weeds. Papá cursed and clenched his teeth each time he plowed. Drops of sweat dribbled down his nose. Trampita and I tired quickly, but we kept on going. We did not want to disappoint Papá. We worked until dark and then went home exhausted.

Sundays, Roberto and the rest of my family went to work. Torito took care of Rubén and Rorra while Mamá joined the rest of us in our battle with the weeds and mud clods. On Saturday nights Roberto and I did not go out. We stayed home to study. During that time, I barely kept up with my schoolwork. My social studies and English classes suffered, and so did my math. I sat in the fifth seat for three weeks in a row.

But when we saw tiny white flowers sprouting from a few plants, we felt our work had paid off. The white petals fell to the ground like snowflakes, leaving a small green bulb, which turned into a strawberry within days. Like children looking for Easter eggs, we searched for strawberries hidden between the leaves. We picked them gently, trying not to bruise them, and placed them in a cardboard crate anchored on a small wooden cart shaped like a horse, which we pushed in front of us as we picked on our knees.

We were disappointed when we came across several plants that had not grown at all. They had no flowers or fruit. As time went by they dried up and died. Other plants began to turn brown, leaving brown patches throughout the field. Joe and other sharecroppers went to see the rancher to tell him what was happening. The rancher examined a few plants and said he thought a blight had infested the plants. He hired a chemical company to fumigate the fields.

The day the chemical company came, Roberto and I missed school to help with the fumigation. We covered the field with huge sheets of white plastic and sealed the edges with dirt. After the wind died down, a chemical gas was pumped in through a hose from a metal tank loaded on the bed of a large truck. Roberto and I walked around the field with shovels, making sure the plastic sheets were completely sealed. We used flashlights to find our way. As the night wore on, I had a hard time keeping my eyes open. I felt like lying down and going to sleep, but Roberto and Papá did not let me. "*Ándale*, Panchito," Roberto yelled out, banging his shovel on the ground. "You can sleep tomorrow when we go home." The fog blew in from the coast and blanketed the fields. To help me keep awake, I imagined myself being stranded on an island and seeking help. I turned my flashlight off and on, hoping to be seen and rescued. The light splintered against the thick gray mist. Roberto went along with the game. He did the same with his flashlight from across the field. By dawn, we were exhausted. Papá's face was as white as the plastic. He was stooped over and had a hard time straightening up. My arms and legs felt like lead. Roberto and I went straight to bed at six o'clock that morning. Papá left to pick strawberries for Ito.

Papá was sure the fumigation had taken care of the problem. He pulled out the dead plants and replaced them with new ones. Every day he examined the dying plants to look for new growth. When he did not see any change, he checked with other sharecroppers: their plants were dying too. The green fields were again covered with dark brown patches. The rancher had the soil tested and found out that the chemicals used to prepare it had been too strong; they had killed the plants.

From that day on, Papá's spirit began to die too. His moods changed from day to day. He began to complain about his back and got angry about everything and everyone, especially Mamá. At times, there was nothing she did that pleased him. He complained to her about work, the kids, the food, the noise, the neighbors. After work, he would throw his black lunch pail on the table, go in his room, and not say a word to anyone. He listened to Mexican music on the radio, smoked, and consumed more aspirin than food. He began to lose weight. "We must be cursed," he said angrily one day after supper. Like Papá, I felt angry and wondered if he was right.

Papá's black mood spilled over into our social life. He did not like Roberto and me to leave the house except for work.

One Saturday night Roberto and I asked his permission to go out. "Where do you want to go?" he asked, looking up at the ceiling. Roberto and I waited for the other to respond. "Where!" he said impatiently.

"To the Vets, Papá," Roberto finally said, looking scared.

"What's that?"

"It's a hall where they have dances," I said, figuring it was my turn to answer.

Papá kept staring into space. Roberto and I stood in front of him with our hands folded in front of us, waiting for a response. There was a long and painful silence. *Why do we have to go through this torture every time we want to go out?* I asked myself. I glanced at Roberto and rolled my eyes.

"Well, are you going to let us go?" I said impatiently. Roberto glanced at me with terror in his eyes and nudged me with his elbow. I knew I had crossed the line.

"I don't like your tone of voice, Pancho. Who do you think you are?" Papá shot back angrily, clenching his teeth and giving me a penetrating look that sent chills up my spine. I lowered my head. My legs began to shake.

"Look at me when I am talking to you!" he said angrily. His words pierced like needles. Mamá must have been listening, because she walked in and broke my silence.

"Let them go, *viejo*. They are good kids; they've never gotten into trouble, even when they lived by themselves," she said softly.

Papá relaxed his jaw and lit a cigarette. "Fine. Roberto can go, but not you, Pancho. You stay home," he said firmly. His eyes were on fire. "And don't you ever talk to me in that tone of voice again, understood?"

"Yes," I responded. My voice cracked. Roberto gave me another nudge. "I am sorry," I added politely.

"No one disrespects me, especially my children," he said. "Be home by midnight. And take the two empty bottles and fill them with water at the gas station on your way back."

I helped Roberto load the two five-gallon bottles that we used for getting our drinking water into the trunk of his car.

"You have to be more patient with Papá," Roberto said.

"I know he's sick, but I am tired of his ugly moods."

"But talking back gets you nowhere," he said. "See, now you can't go with me to the Vets."

"I know," I said sadly.

The bottles rattled in the back of the trunk as my brother left without me. I went back into the house feeling furious with Papá and myself.

Saint Christopher Medal

We had lost our three acres of strawberries, and I felt sad for Papá. But I was also relieved, because I did not have to work late in the evenings and miss days of school anymore. I had more time to study. I caught up in math and took the second seat in the first row. Margie Ito continued to take the first seat. She was unmovable. In social studies I scored ninety-nine percent on the final test on the United States Constitution. I struggled in my English class but always did well on spelling tests, which we had once a week. I wrote the spelling words in my notepad and studied them as I worked.

The hardest task for me was writing a final paper for my science class. We were to pick any science topic, research it, and write a report on it. I had a hard time deciding on a topic. Nothing came to mind. Then one day as I was flipping through a history book, I came across a brief section on Christopher Columbus and the discovery of the New World. As I skimmed it, my eye caught the name Hernán Cortés. I was fascinated. It was the first time I had read about someone with a Spanish name. I read the paragraph several times and said the name Hernán Cortés out loud. I liked the sound of it. His name ended with a "z" sound just like my family's last name. I felt proud. I began to wonder what it was like to be an explorer over four hundred years ago.

Then an idea for my report came to me: I would explore the solar system. I went to the library, checked out books on the moon and the planets, and read them, taking notes. I created a story about a group of six scientists who decide to explore part of the solar system. The scientists were Roberto and I, cocaptains; and Trampita, Torito, Rorra, and Rubén, our assistants. We built a spaceship and traveled to seven planets and the moon. We explored each planet, in order of increasing distance from the sun: Mercury, Venus, Mars, Jupiter, Saturn, Neptune, and Pluto. I kept a journal on our explorations and made drawings to illustrate our findings. Mr. Milo, also my science teacher, gave me an A+ on the report, even though I had made several grammatical mistakes in it. He told me I had a good imagination and said he had displayed my report at Open House the night before. I did not know what he meant by Open House, and I was more confused when he said he missed meeting my parents on that evening.

A few days before the end of the school year, our class practiced for graduation in the auditorium, which also served as the cafeteria. We lined up outside in the corridor in alphabetical order and marched in to music played on a record player. We walked up the stairs to the stage, where we sat in cold metal chairs. We repeated this exercise several times until we got it right. We were told to wear dark pants and a white shirt. Girls were to wear a white blouse and dark skirt.

All day Saturday, I kept thinking about graduation. I was excited about leaving El Camino Junior High School and starting Santa Maria High School on time in the fall. When Papá and I got home from work at six o'clock, Mamá had already heated water in a pot for my bath. I washed my hair with Fab detergent and scrubbed my hands extra hard with Ajax to get rid of the strawberry stains. I put on a clean pair of jeans and a white T-shirt. "You can't wear that T-shirt, *mijo,*" Mamá cried out. "It's yellowish and frayed."

"It's the best one I have."

"Here, Panchito, wear this one. It's whiter than yours," Roberto said, handing me one of his T-shirts. I tried it on. It was a little big, but it was better than the one I had. "You look pretty good," he said, chuckling. "All you need are a few more muscles like me to fill it."

"Thanks, Mr. Atlas," I said, laughing.

"You'd better hurry. It's getting late," Mamá said. She

rubbed Tres Rosas oil in my hair and helped me comb it. Papá, who was in a rare good mood, splashed some of his Old Spice aftershave lotion on my face. His large, callused hands felt like old leather gloves.

"I don't want you to smell like rotten strawberries," he said, smiling. "If you smell like me, nobody will want to get near you." He took off his Saint Christopher medal, which he wore around his neck, and handed it to me. "Here, *mijo*," he said, " I want you to have this. It will guide you."

"*Gracias*, Papá," I said, admiring the worn-out image between my fingers. The medal was linked to a chain similar to the pull-cord attached to the light bulb hanging in the middle of our kitchen. Papá had worn the medal ever since I could remember. "Are you sure you want to give it to me?"

"Of course," he answered. "It's your present for finishing the eighth grade." He stood up slowly and hugged me. I noticed the necklace had left a white ring around his sunburned neck.

"You'd better get going!" Mamá insisted, giving Roberto and me a slight shove. "May God bless you."

Roberto and I arrived at El Camino Junior High School a few minutes late. I ran down the corridor looking for my spot in line. My classmates were already waiting. I saw Robert Lindsay and moved in front of him. I was glad to see that he was wearing a T-shirt too, because most of the boys were wearing collared white shirts. They looked like penguins. Mr. McEacheron, the P.E. coach, walked up and down the hall, trying to keep us from making too much noise. Parents and friends milled around the cafeteria, waiting for the ceremony to start. As soon as we heard the music, we quieted down and began the procession. When we entered the auditorium, I spotted Roberto in the audience. I imagined Papá and Mamá sitting next to him, their faces glowing as my name was called to receive my diploma.

Summer Skirmishes

The summer after graduation from junior high was pretty much the same as those of previous years, except that I was the only one who joined Papá in picking strawberries for Ito. Roberto came only on Saturdays and Sundays because he worked full-time as a janitor for the Santa Maria school district. I looked forward to weekends, when my brother, Papá, and I worked together. Roberto and I found ways to have fun. We raced to see who could pick faster and fill more crates. He was a much faster picker than I was, so I lost every time, except when Papá helped me. Whenever Papá and I picked side by side, he handed me handfuls of strawberries. Papá never let on that he knew about our game, but I figured he must have known, because one time when I filled my crate faster than Roberto he glanced at my brother and winked at me.

One morning I started a strawberry war. I had learned the spelling and definition of the word *skirmish,* which I had added to my notepad to memorize that day. I was bored and tired of picking on my knees, so I stood up to stretch. Roberto was ahead of me, two rows away. I could not resist the perfect target. I picked up a rotten strawberry, looked around to make sure Papá was not looking, and threw it at Roberto. The mushy bullet splashed on his back, leaving a reddish, purplish wound the size of a baseball. My brother turned around, startled. He knew I was the enemy when he saw me snickering. He raised his clenched fist at me, turned back, and kept on picking.

I glanced at Ito. He had a puzzled look on his face but did not say anything. *I hope he didn't see me,* I thought. I continued working and, to keep my mind occupied, began whistling rock 'n' roll tunes and daydreaming about Peggy and the Vets. I danced song after song with her. Suddenly I felt a blow on the back of my right shoulder. I instinctively reached behind with my left hand and scooped up a rotten strawberry. I turned around. Roberto was picking on his knees behind me, four rows away. He had his head down, trying to hide his smirk. At lunchtime Roberto and I put on our jackets to hide our strawberry stains.

When we got home, we quickly took off our shirts. Mamá saw the stains, shook her head, and gave us a stern look. I knew she would not tell Papá because she did not want to upset him.

That evening, Ito was coming to our house to deliver our paychecks for the week. I was afraid he might have seen me throw the strawberry at Roberto and say something to Papá. I was terribly nervous.

In preparation for his visit, we all made sure the house was in order. Roberto swept and wet-mopped the floors. I cleaned the kitchen. Trampita and Torito picked up papers and trash outside the house that dogs had scattered from the garbage cans. Rorra followed them, making sure they did not miss anything. Mamá made a fresh batch of flour tortillas and refried beans to give to Ito. Papá sat at the kitchen table, giving orders and going over our savings, which he kept in a small metal box.

Ito arrived shortly after we had finished our chores. He was dressed up as usual, in khaki pants and shirt and brown shoes. His dark, straight hair was combed back, and his tan face looked smooth and shiny. I fixed my eyes on every move he made and hung on every word he said, trying to see if he was upset with me. He and Papá shook hands and bowed. Ito took a seat at the head of the table, took out his checkbook, and placed it in front of him. Mamá offered him *taquitos*. "No, *gracias*," he said in a thick American accent.

There were long periods of silence, because Ito spoke only English and Papá spoke only Spanish. Mamá, Roberto, and I interpreted for both of them. Ito began to write the three checks. I knew Papá's check was for sixty-five dollars, because he got paid a dollar an hour. Roberto and I received eighty-five cents per hour, just like the *braceros*. Ito paid Papá more than us because Papá was a better picker and because he had worked for Ito for several summers. Papá felt special and looked for ways to show Ito his gratitude. When it was time to quit work at the end of the day, Papá kept on picking for another ten or fifteen minutes even though he did not receive pay for the extra time.

When Ito finished making out the checks, he handed them to Papá.

"Pregúntale si quiere algo para tomar," Papá said, bowing his head and smiling.

"Papá asked if you would like something to drink," I said.

"No, gracias, Don Francisco," Ito responded, bowing to Papá.

"I made some *taquitos* for you to take home," Mamá said proudly. She handed Ito a bundle of refried bean tacos wrapped in waxed paper. Ito's eyes lit up.

"My wife and kids love your tacos," he said.

"Don Gabriel really liked Mamá's *taquitos* too," I said. "Remember him, Mr. Ito?"

"Of course I remember him," Ito responded. "He worked for me a few years ago. Díaz, the labor contractor, had it in for him and sent him back to Mexico." Ito paused, looked straight into my eyes, and, raising his voice, added,

"He was a good, serious worker." I lowered my head. Ito looked at his watch and excused himself. Papá and Mamá walked him to the door. I followed behind. He got in his pickup truck, waved, and said, chuckling: "You have a good arm, Panchito." I blushed and looked away.

"What did he say?" Papá asked.

"He said Panchito is a good worker," Mamá responded, coming to my rescue.

I looked up at Mamá and smiled sheepishly.

On weekdays, after work, Roberto and I regularly went to the city dump with Trampita and Torito to look for discarded treasures, like wood, paint, and broken toys. On one of our trips I found an old copy of *Dr. Doolittle*. I tried reading five pages every evening, but often I was too tired to concentrate and did not understand what I read. Other times my younger brothers played kick-the-can in front of our barrack and tried to get me to play with them, but I refused because Carlos, a bully, never allowed my friend Manuelito to play too.

Roberto did not play games outside with the boys. Papá said he was too old to play sports. So he worked on his car. He kept it spotless and shiny.

Sometimes Trampita and I watched tadpoles and little fish in the nearby reservoir. Trampita came up with a plan one day to catch fish and sell them for a nickel apiece to kids in our neighborhood. It took us a few evenings after work to finish the project. The first day we made a trip to the city dump to look for empty glass jars to put the fish in and for materials to build a stand. We found old splintered boards, two-by-fours, and cardboard. The following evening we began construction under the watchful eye of Carlos and his two friends, who played all day. They seemed fascinated by our skills. We cleaned the wood, pulling out rusty nails and rubbing the boards together to smooth out the splinters. The third day, Roberto helped us build a stand. We then covered it with cardboard and hung a sign that read GOLDFISH, 5¢ EACH.

The next step was to catch fish. We walked to the reservoir, which looked like a barren hill. It was at the edge of the two-lane road leading to Santa Maria, about a quarter of a mile from Bonetti Ranch. An old, lonely pepper tree stood guard next to it. Its lower branches slumped to the ground, bent from the weight of kids who swung on them, playing cowboys and Indians. Trampita yanked off two of its broken branches and gave me one. Carrying the branch in one hand and an empty coffee can and a glass jar in the other, we stepped back a few yards from the base of the reservoir to gain speed and ran up to the top, which was about five feet wide all around. We took off our shoes, rolled up our pants, and carefully slid down the crater to the edge of the water. Using our branches, we cleared the algae and removed empty beer bottles, crushed cans, and paper. We threw in tortilla bits, trying to attract the little gray fish and goldfish that hid under murky waters. Hundreds of tadpoles squirted around, but no fish. We waited and waited. Nothing.

That evening we went home empty-handed and disappointed, but we did not give up. The next day we returned to the same spot. We sprinkled the clearing with fresh tortilla bits and waited. I kissed my Saint Christopher medal. The croaking sound of frogs broke the silence, and within seconds a swarm of tadpoles followed by a pair of goldfish filled the clearing. I could feel my heart thumping faster and faster. I gently put the can in the water and quickly scooped it up, catching one of the fish and several tadpoles. "I got one!" I yelled out. Trampita darted over excitedly. He put his hand in the can and carefully grabbed the tiny goldfish and put it in the jar. Holding the container steady, we climbed back up to the top and placed it on the ground. We lay on our stomachs, facing each other with the jar between our faces, and watched the little fish swim rapidly up and down and around. My brother's face looked huge. He opened and closed his lips rapidly, pretending to be a fish, and chuckled. I stuck out my tongue and made faces. We both burst out laughing.

"We'd better catch a few more before it gets dark," I said, still laughing. We went back, caught nine more fish, and skipped home, whistling. As we reached Bonetti Ranch and turned the corner, we ran into Carlos and his two friends. They were standing behind a large wooden box in front of an empty barrack. On the wall behind the stand was a sign: GOLDFISH, 2 FOR 5¢.

From that day on, I spent more time struggling through *Dr. Doolittle*.

Toward the end of the summer, when the peak of the strawberry season was over and when work was slow, Ito gave us Saturday afternoons off. Papá took advantage of one of those afternoons to try his new hair clippers on my younger brothers and me. He found the old rusty pair at the city dump. The right handle was broken and a few teeth were missing. Papá oiled it and set up his barbershop in the shed, using an unstable wooden box as a chair.

I was his first customer. I stripped to my waist and climbed onto the box. Papá began to cut with his new tool. As he clipped, hair fell on my shoulders, pricking me like needles. I squirmed and wiped it off. The box creaked. I moved again. Papá quickly moved the clippers away from my head and yelled, "Don't move!" It was too late. A chunk of hair fell on my lap. I reached up to feel the nicked spot. "I said stay still!" Papá yelled again, slapping my hand. Using his left hand like a vice, he held my head still and clipped away with his right. As he cut, he put more and more weight on his left hand, making my neck twist to the right. It felt as though he was trying to push me into the ground. I tried to straighten it, pushing up against my Papá's hand. The box creaked. Another clump

of hair rolled down my shoulders. Tears came to my eyes.
I clenched my teeth and clasped my hands together until
it was over. I climbed off the crate, rushed to the bedroom, and picked up the hand mirror. I slowly scanned
my face, wiping away the hair clippings from my chin and
nose. As I brought the mirror upward to my forehead, I
closed my eyes, said a silent prayer, and quickly opened
them. I was shocked. My front wave was gone. I had short
bangs and nicks on both sides. I looked like the stray dogs
with mange that populated Bonetti Ranch. I felt like
yelling at Papá, but I knew I couldn't. It would be worse.
I complained to Mamá.

"You don't look too bad, *mijo,*" she said tenderly. "In a
couple of weeks it'll grow back." She picked up my cap
and put it on me. "There, you look just fine," she added
cheerfully.

I knew Mamá did not mean it because she bought Papá
a new set of clippers at the Goodwill Store the following
week. I wore my cap all the time for days and only took it
off when I went to bed. I skipped going to the Vets dances
with Roberto for the rest of the summer.

Becoming a Saint

I could hardly contain myself. It was Sunday, September third, the last day of work before school started. Tomorrow I would start my freshman year at Santa Maria High School on the first day of classes. I would not have to move to Fresno to pick grapes and cotton and miss school for two and a half months. My shoulders felt light even though I was tired.

"I have never seen you so happy, *mijo*," Mamá said when we got home from work.

"He's excited because he gets to ride to school with me," Roberto said, slapping me on the back.

My brother was going into his junior year. He should have graduated last year, but, like me, he had failed first grade because he did not speak English well enough. He fell behind another year because he missed so much school. Every year, for nine years, he started school some-time in January, after the cotton season was over.

"He kept right up with me the whole day," Roberto said. "I couldn't believe it. What did you put in his tacos?"

"Same thing I put in yours," she responded, chuckling. "*Puros frijoles.*"

"That explains it," Roberto said laughing. "Beans will do it every time."

That evening I tried reading a few more pages of *Dr. Doolittle*, but I could not focus. I put the book down and laid out on the bed the clothes I was going to wear for school: a new pair of tan corduroy pants, a white T-shirt, and a light brown sleeveless vest with black buttons. Roberto suggested that I wear blue jeans because most boys wore them in high school, but I did not want to wear the same type of pants I wore to work. I took a bath and scrubbed my hands with bleach to get rid of the straw-berry stains. I whistled and sang, forgetting that my brothers had to take a bath too. "Are you stuck in there?" Roberto shouted, knocking on the shed door several times. I quickly stepped out of the tub, dried myself, and put on my underwear and pants. "It's about time, Pan-chito," my brother said as I walked passed him. "Your hands look like prunes."

The next morning I got up extra early to get ready for school. I wore my Saint Christopher medal outside my

T-shirt to show it off. Papá walked by me without saying a word and went outside to warm up the DeSoto to go to work. He looked tired and sad. The dark circles under his eyes were darker than usual, and he had not bothered to shave. He hardly touched his breakfast. He grabbed his black lunch pail from the table, glanced at Roberto and me, and left. "What's wrong with Papá?" I asked. "I haven't seen him this sad all summer."

"He's in one of his bad moods, *mijo*," Mamá said. "He's gotten worse ever since our strawberry acres were ruined. You know that. He complained all night about his back and took several aspirins, but they didn't seem to help. He's also upset because you boys are not going to work with him. He hates working alone."

"Sometimes I think he doesn't like us to go to school," I said.

"Oh, he does, Panchito," Mamá said. "Why do you say that?"

"The other night when I was reading *Dr. Doolittle*, Papá asked me why I liked school so much. I told him I liked learning and wanted to be a teacher. And do you know what he said?"

"What?" Roberto asked.

"He said, 'Don't be stupid. Only rich people become teachers.' He walked away before I had a chance to say anything. He made me really mad."

"I am glad you didn't say anything," Roberto said.

"When he's in a bad mood, it's better not to talk to him."

"But maybe he was testing you," Mamá said. "Sometimes he says things to make you think. You know how he is."

"Well, he made me mad," I repeated.

"Hey, we'd better get going. It's getting late," Roberto said, glancing at the clock. As my brother and I drove on South Broadway on our way to Santa Maria High School, I felt the same as I had when I started first grade: excited but nervous. I watched the reflection of Roberto's 1953 green Buick on the storefront windows along the way. The car looked like a fish in a bowl. At times it appeared large and long, and at other times it looked small and scrunched. I recalled taking this same route in the Border Patrol car, the year before, to pick up Roberto. *A lot of things happened to us in less than a year,* I thought. *I wonder what this year will be like.*

Roberto parked the car in the student parking lot, behind the boys' gym, next to the football field. The lot was filling up quickly with cars that looked like large insects. Some were lowered in the front and painted in bright metallic colors, like candy apple red, and had tucked and rolled upholstery in white or black. I followed other incoming freshmen into Wilson Gym, which smelled like dirty socks. I had never seen so many students. We filled the bleachers on both sides of the gym. A red and white banner with the school's motto, "Enter to Learn, Go Forth to Serve," hung from the ceiling. The principal gave us information about the school and our schedule of classes. He then introduced the student body president, who welcomed us and told us that our school mascot was a saint. He informed us that we would be known as the Class of 1962 of the Santa Maria High School Saints. I liked the sound of it, and I knew Mamá would too. We were also told that classes would officially start the following day and that we should meet with our counselor to discuss our class schedule.

After the meeting I asked for directions to the administration building and rushed to see my counselor, Mr. Kinkade. I ran across campus, noticing many old buildings with red tile roofs. They reminded me of some of the houses in Tlaquepaque, the small town in Mexico where I was born. Tile corridors with arches that looked onto a large courtyard with beautiful gardens connected the buildings in the oldest part of campus. My counselor's office was in the old main administration building, next to the attendance office. I went through one of the long corridors to get to it.

Mr. Kinkade sat at his desk, which was piled with folders and papers. Behind him was a tall, dark brown bookcase full of thick binders and books. To his left was a window that looked out onto the courtyard. He was dressed in a gray suit and a light blue bow tie. His thick hair was peppered with white and combed back. After he introduced himself, he picked up a folder with my name on it and said, "I see you graduated from El Camino Junior High School. Have you thought of what you want to do after high school?" Before I had a chance to answer, he added, "We have excellent vocational programs in car mechanics, electronics, and wood shop. We also have a program for future farmers."

"I'd like to be a teacher," I responded, thinking about Mr. Lema, my sixth-grade teacher, who had helped me with English during the lunch hours when I was far behind in my class because I had missed so many weeks of school.

"Oh, I see," he said, straightening up and leaning forward. "So you're planning to go to college."

"College?" I said.

"Yes, college," he said, amused. "You need to go to college to be a teacher. It's five years of study beyond high school. It can be expensive."

Maybe that's what Papá meant when he said only rich people became teachers, I thought.

"But," he quickly added, "if you get excellent grades, you can get scholarships."

"Scholarships?" I did not know what the word meant.

"It's gift money given to students with excellent grades to attend college."

I perked up. "So, if I get good grades, I can get free money to go to college?" I wanted to make sure I'd heard him right.

"That's correct," he said. He opened the folder and ran his index finger down the page. "I see you have good grades, especially in math, but your grades in English are not as good," he said.

"I know," I said apologetically. "But I am working on it."

"Good. Now, let's see here," he said, looking at my schedule. "Let's substitute typing for wood shop and put you in an algebra class." He handed me the revised schedule and added, "You're set."

"Thank you very much," I said, shaking his hand. I walked out of his office feeling less nervous about school and more excited than ever.

The following day, when I got to my first P.E. class, I was surprised to see my teacher dressed in red shorts. *Men don't wear shorts,* I said to myself. He also wore a white T-shirt and white tennis shoes. He was short and slim and had a crewcut. Around his neck hung a whistle, which he used to get our attention instead of calling us by name. He emphasized our being on time and suiting up. Suiting up meant having to buy a uniform just like his and wearing it for P.E. every day. I hated having to wear shorts as much as I had disliked having to wear suspenders when I was in elementary school. But I had no choice. If we did not suit up right, we would lose points, which hurt our grade.

The coach walked us to the locker room, assigned us

a locker for our gym clothes, and showed us the shower room. He informed us that at the end of every class period we had to take a shower. Everyone moaned except me. I was excited. Roberto had told me about how great it was to take showers at school. He even brought his own soap. I decided to bring my own soap too. This part made up for having to wear shorts.

My last period in the morning was typing. The classroom was off a dark hall, on the south side of the school. Small, framed windows covered the wall facing Main Street School and on the opposite wall hung long and narrow blackboards. There were several rows of tables with typewriters, spaced out every three feet.

In contrast to my P.E. coach, the typing teacher was well dressed. He had on a blue suit with wide lapels and a white and blue striped tie, and he wore a gold ring on the little finger of his right hand. He paced up and down in front of the classroom, explaining what he expected of us. "In this class you're not only going to learn to type," he said, "you're also going to learn to be fast and accurate. Your grade will be based on speed and accuracy. I would suggest you practice typing at home or come here after school." *How am I going to practice?* I thought. *We don't have a typewriter at home, and I have to work after school.* I went through my other classes worrying about typing class.

I liked my social studies and algebra classes in the afternoon. My social studies teacher, Mrs. Dorothy Taylor, was a small, thin woman with short, curly hair and light blue eyes. She used a lot of make-up. After telling us about the class, she showed us a black-and-white film about a teenager who argues with his father. The boy wants to go out with his friends on a school night, but his father does not let him. The father picks up his son's books, shoves them at him, and tells him to go to his room and study. The son throws the books on the floor, runs to his room, and slams the door shut. Mrs. Taylor moved around the room quickly, like a mosquito, encouraging us to talk about the film. The class thought the son was wrong for throwing the books, but they agreed that it was okay for him to argue with his father. I thought it was strange, because at home we were taught that it was disrespectful to argue with our parents, especially our father. If we disagreed with Papá, we kept our opinions to ourselves. I did not say anything in class, but I thought a lot about it.

I went to algebra, my last-period class, feeling confident because I had always done well in math. My teacher, Mr. Ivan Coe, was a tall, wiry man. His small brown eyes darted around the room and he took quick, short steps like a duck. He told us he had an excellent memory and proved it by taking roll and then calling each one of us by name without looking at his roll sheet. He then asked us to give him double-digit numbers up to twenty to multiply in his head. He shot back the answers instantly, never making a mistake. Like our typing teacher, Mr. Coe said he would grade us on speed and accuracy. He promised to give us pop quizzes once a week and to return the results the following day. As an example, he gave us a fifteen-minute math exam and had us correct it in class. I did well. After his class, I decided to write down double-digit multiplication tables on postcards and memorize them while I worked. I wanted to be as good as Mr. Coe.

If the Shoe Fits

The class in which I thought it would be the easiest to get a good grade, P.E., turned out to be one of the hardest. I was preparing for the physical fitness test at the end of the quarter, doing push-ups, sit-ups, and chin-ups, and climbing ropes, running sprints, and lifting weights. I was doing fine, until the day it happened.

I was running a few minutes late that morning. When I got to the locker room, my classmates were already getting dressed in their gym clothes. I was in such a hurry that the foul smell of dirty socks and sweaty T-shirts did not bother me. I rushed to my locker, elbowing my way through, and began opening the combination lock with one hand and unbuttoning my shirt with the other. I unhooked the lock, flung the door open, quickly grabbed my gym clothes, and discovered my tennis shoes were missing. I checked inside again. Nothing. I put on my shorts and T-shirt and ran outside and lined up with the rest of my class. The coach blew his whistle. "You're late," he shouted, looking me up and down. "Why aren't you wearing your tennis shoes?"

"I couldn't find them, Coach," I responded, holding back my tears. "They're gone from my locker."

"Well, you'd better find them. It'll cost you five points each time you don't suit up completely."

At the end of the period, I checked in my locker again and looked all around the locker room. I was out of luck. I did not even enjoy taking a shower that day or going to classes. When I got home that evening after work, I told Papá and Mamá about it. "Maybe you didn't put them back in the locker," Mamá said.

"No, I am sure I did."

"Maybe you didn't and someone picked them up," Roberto said. "Did you check in the lost and found?"

"Yes, I checked everywhere."

"Well, if you can't find them, we'll have to buy you a new pair," Mamá said.

"But it won't be until the end of next week, when Roberto gets paid," Papá added, biting his lower lip.

My heart sank. *There goes my grade*, I thought. I went outside, stood underneath the pepper tree next to the outhouse, and cried silently.

I did not suit up for P.E. for the next few days. Then one evening, when Roberto and I got home from work, Trampita and Torito ran up to me. Trampita was snickering and hiding something behind his back. "Look what we got!" he exclaimed, dangling a pair of worn and soiled tennis shoes in front of me. "We found them in the dump," Torito said proudly.

I excitedly tried them on, turning my head away from them to avoid the foul smell. "They're too big," I said, disappointed.

"Try them with two pairs of socks," Mamá said. "They'll fit better."

I went to the dresser and pulled out the thickest pair of socks I could find and put them on. I slipped on the tennis shoes and paced around the kitchen. "They're still a bit loose. But they feel better," I said. Trampita's and Torito's eyes lit up.

I soaked an old rag in a pot of hot water and scrubbed them. The steam made them smell worse, and when I finished, they were more gray than white. I placed them outside on the stairs overnight to dry and air out. The next morning, at P.E., I lined up for roll call fully dressed and happy not to lose five more points.

A few days later, my feet began to itch. I told the coach and he said I might have athlete's foot. I thought it was a compliment until I found out what it really meant. I took off the two layers of socks and I noticed I had cracked, blistered, and peeling areas between the toes. This lasted a long time, even after I got a new pair of tennis shoes. I ended up getting a C in P.E. at mid-semester.

A Promotion

During the fall, Papá's depression got worse. Work in the fields was scarce, and when he finally found a job thinning lettuce, he lasted only a few days because of his back pain. He wore a wide belt for support, and when he could no longer stoop over, he worked on his knees until his back gave out completely. The pay from Roberto's part-time janitorial job and our earnings working in the fields on weekends were not enough to get us through. Roberto got paid twice a month, and every other week Mamá had to cut back on groceries. Once in a while Papá did some light work for Bonetti, the owner of the ranch, to help pay the rent, but as time passed we fell further and further behind on the monthly payments. "It's a disgrace not paying the rent on time," Papá said one evening as he opened our empty metal box. "It's a shame!" He banged his fist on the kitchen table. A glass flew off, hit the floor, and broke. Trampita and Torito got scared and ran out of the house.

"Calm down, *viejo*," Mamá said. Looking worried, she dried her hands on her apron and placed them on Papá's shoulders.

"How can I?" he said, shrugging her hands away. "This life is for the dogs. No, it's worse. Dogs can at least seek out their food. I can't even do that." He slowly got up from the table and hobbled to his room. Mamá gave us a pained look, shook her head, and followed him, trying to console him.

"I have to get an extra job," Roberto said, slumping in his chair and lowering his head. "I don't know what else to do."

"Can't you get Papá a job where you work?" I asked. "I could help you both after school."

"I've already tried. Mr. Sims told me they already have a full-time janitor and me."

As usual, at the end of the school day, Roberto and I met in the parking lot and headed for Main Street Elementary School. We drove down Broadway, passing students who filled the sidewalks like colorful ants in a parade. A few couples strolled holding hands, talking, and laughing. As we turned the corner onto Main Street, Roberto made a sharp turn and parked next to an old, beat-up yellow van that had Santa Maria Window Cleaners signs on its panels. "I've seen that guy before," Roberto said, pointing to a man who had just finished washing the outside windows of Kress, the five-and-dime store. The man tucked the squeegee and chamois in his back pant pocket, picked up the bucket and brush, and headed toward the van. He was a short, stocky man dressed in khaki pants and a short-sleeved shirt, half tucked in.

"Hi," my brother said nervously as the man loaded the equipment in the back of the truck. "My name is Roberto."

"I am Mike Nevel," the man said in a deep, raspy voice.

"I was wondering... do you need any help?" Roberto asked.

The man spat on the curb and adjusted his soiled pants. "You mean, am I hiring?"

"Yes," Roberto replied.

"I could use someone on a part-time basis. Do you have any experience?"

"Oh, it's not for me," Roberto responded. "It's for my dad. He needs a job."

"Has he done janitorial work?"

"No, but he is a good worker," Roberto said proudly.

"Well, I'll have to meet him and talk to him."

"He doesn't speak English," I said. "Only Spanish."

"Can't use him. In this business I need someone who can speak English and with experience. What about you?" he said, pointing at Roberto.

"My brother already has a job," I said. "I have experience. I've been helping him clean Main Street School."

"You're too young, son," he said looking me up and down and chuckling. He then turned to Roberto and continued: "So you have experience at Main Street School..."

"I am a janitor there, part-time," Roberto said.

"What about weekends? Do you work there on weekends?"

"No, just on weekdays."

"What about working for me on weekends? I can pay you $1.25 an hour."

"Sure," Roberto responded immediately.

"What about me?" I asked. "I can work with him."

"You can help if you want, but I can't pay you." When he saw our long faces, he quickly added, "Okay, if he works out, I'll pay him. But only if he works out."

"I'll work out," I said confidently.

For the next four weekends, Roberto and I worked with Mike Nevel, cleaning offices and washing windows. The first day, Mike worked closely with us, showing us what to clean and observing how well we worked. Roberto showed me how to use the twenty-inch floor-scrubbing machine. I had a hard time learning to control it. Luckily, the machine had a rubber strip around its base and every time I bumped into a baseboard, the machine bounced back, giving me a slight jolt in protest. Eventually Mike Nevel let Roberto and me do the work by ourselves. Every Saturday and Sunday, my brother and I drove to Mike

Nevel's house on West Donovan to pick up the keys and the truck.

One Saturday evening when we returned the van, Mike Nevel invited us in. He introduced us to his wife, a friendly, petite woman who also had a raspy voice. Roberto and I sat on a large couch across from Mike, who sat on a reclining chair. His wife sat on a matching sofa chair next to him and smoked a cigarette.

"How are things going?" Mike asked, lighting a half-smoked cigar.

"Fine," we responded at the same time. Roberto reached into his pocket and took out a ring full of keys and handed them to Mike.

"No, you keep them," Mike said. "I have an extra set." Roberto and I looked at each other and smiled. Mike brought his reclining chair to a sitting position, took a puff, and said to me: "I am getting too old and tired of working evenings during the week. How would you like to take over for me? I'll pay you a buck an hour."

"Sure!" I blurted out excitedly.

"You'll be cleaning a few of the same places you and Roberto have been cleaning on weekends: the gas company, the savings and loan, and Betty's Fabrics every day and Twitchel and Twitchel, a lawyers' office, once a week, on Wednesdays. You won't have to strip and wax the floors or wash the windows. You'll continue doing that on weekends."

Roberto and I thanked him and went home excited. *Papá will be proud of us*, I thought.

Papá was happy when Roberto and I told him about my new job, but his good mood did not last long. That Saturday night he got angry with Roberto and me because we came home from the movies past midnight. "Don't think just because you give me your paychecks that you can do whatever you want," he said firmly.

"But we're only a few minutes late," I said, recalling the discussion we had in Mrs. Taylor's class about the film in which a boy argues with his father.

"Don't you dare talk back!" he said, raising his voice. "I am still the man in charge of this house. You must obey and respect me, or else!"

Roberto and I went to our room, said our prayers, and went to bed. As I lay in bed I thought how lucky I was to be going to school and to have a job. I did not enjoy being at home when Papá was in a bad mood.

All day Monday I was excited to start my new job. After my last class, I went to the public library on Broadway and worked on my homework. I did my math first because I liked it best. At five o'clock, when the offices closed, I walked a few more blocks to the gas company, which was on West Main Street. It was a huge building with a front office that connected to a large back structure two stories high. As I opened the door to the rear entrance, a draft of warm air hit my face. It felt safe and comfortable. I went to the janitor's room, picked up the cleaning cart, and began cleaning the offices on the first floor. I emptied the wastebaskets and feather-dusted the desks, which were piled with scattered papers. They looked like my high school counselor's desk. I wiped the ashtrays with a wet rag and straightened the papers.

I then went upstairs to the second floor. It was one large room set up like an auditorium. In front of the room was a full kitchen. Above the stove was a mirror, angled so that people sitting in the audience could view the top of the range. A plate of cookies sat on the counter with a handwritten note that read PLEASE HELP YOURSELF. The following day, the plate of cookies was still there. No one had touched them. By the end of the week, someone had changed the note. It read JANITOR, PLEASE HELP YOUR-SELF. After I finished cleaning the bathrooms and dust-mopping the floors, I took a handful of cookies and went downstairs.

I sat at one of the desks to do my homework. I read the first two chapters in my English text, *Myths and Their Meaning*. I had a hard time understanding them. I put the book down, ate more cookies, and wondered what the person who sat at the desk did all day. *It must be neat to work in an office*, I thought. I noticed a picture frame partially hidden behind a pile of folders and picked it up.

It was a color photograph of a boy dressed in a football uniform and a man standing next to him, smiling proudly with his arm around the boy. I figured it was the boy's father. I placed the photo in front of the pile of papers and reread the first chapter until Roberto came by to pick me up to go home.

A Typing Machine

By mid-semester, my typing speed had improved, but not my accuracy. The teacher gave us weekly typing quizzes. He projected words that flashed on a screen as fast as a blink of an eye, and we had to type them just as fast. I managed to keep up, but when he moved on to short complete sentences, I kept making mistakes. To get an A in the course, I had to type fifty-five words a minute with no errors. I needed more practice typing. I found the answer to my problem in a lawyers' office.

On Wednesday evening, after I finished the gas company, I went to clean Twitchel and Twitchel, an attorneys' office. It was a long, one-story building with several offices, located a few blocks from Main Street. The building had wall-to-wall carpeting, dark wood paneling, and shelves full of thick, leather-bound books. It had a storage room with stacks of long sheets of paper with numbers on the margins and boxes of pens, pencils, staples, and paper clips. An old typewriter full of cobwebs sat on the floor in a corner. I picked it up, placed it on top of a cabinet, and dusted it. I loaded it with a sheet of paper and tried typing on it. The keys were sluggish and the letters were barely visible. As I set it back down, I heard the front door open and someone say, "Who's here?"

"It's nobody," I responded, quickly coming out of the storage room. "It's just me, the janitor."

"Hi," he said. "I am Bob Twitchel. Mike Nevel told me about you. I didn't expect you to be so young."

"Glad to meet you, sir," I responded. "My name is Francisco."

"Good to meet you," he said. "I'll be here only a few minutes." He went into his office and left the door open. I passed by and glanced in. He was talking on the phone. After I dusted, I cleaned the bathroom and began vacuuming. When I finished, I wound the cord and placed the vacuum in the storage room. I looked at the typewriter again. *It's not being used,* I thought. *Maybe he'll sell it to me cheap.* I passed by Mr. Twitchel's office and glanced in again. His eyes caught mine. I stood in front of the door, feeling nervous. "What is it?" he asked, putting down his pen.

"The old typewriter," I said. "The one in the storage room..."

"Oh, that old clunker. I've been meaning to get rid of it," he said. "Why do you ask?"

"Well, would you sell it to me?" I asked, feeling more at ease.

"Sell it! You can have it," he responded, chuckling. "I was going to throw it away."

"Thank you," I said excitedly. Then I remembered Papá telling us to avoid owing anybody anything, including favors. "I'd rather buy it from you," I added.

"Let's take a look at it," he said, looking a bit puzzled. I brought it out from the storage room and placed it on his desk. He examined it. "It needs a new ribbon."

"Yes, I know," I said.

He gave me a surprised look, smiled, and said: "I'll tell you what. Get a new ribbon for it from the storage room and give me five bucks."

"Thank you! I don't have the money with me, but I'll bring it to you by the end of the month."

"Whenever you can—no hurry."

I took the typewriter home and practiced on the kitchen table every night after work. My younger brothers and sister complained about the noise because they could not sleep, so I placed a towel underneath it to keep the clatter down. Mamá was pleased when I told her I got an excellent grade in typing. "You're a typing machine, *mijo*," she said, chuckling. "You got fast fingers from picking strawberries and cotton."

Making Connections

At the end of my freshman year, I received good grades in all subjects except English, even though I had worked the hardest in it. Writing was difficult for me. My freshman English teacher told me that my writing was weak. She suggested that I read more, that reading would improve my writing. "At least read the newspaper every day," she told me. "Read for enjoyment." I had little time to read. I read only for information for my classes, and I could barely keep up. Besides, we had no reading material at home and we didn't get the newspaper. I never got more free time to read all during high school, but I did learn to read for enjoyment. It happened in my sophomore year, in English class.

Miss Audrey Bell, my teacher, had a reputation for being hard. When she walked into the class the first day and wrote her name on the board, I heard moans from classmates sitting next to me. "I am sunk!" one of them said. "Hello, F," another uttered. Now I was even more worried.

Miss Bell had a round face, a small turned-up nose, full lips, and lively blue eyes, and she wore wire-rimmed glasses. Her smile never left her, even when she was upset. When she wrote on the board, her upper arm shook like jelly, just like Mamá's arms. The back of her hands were covered with small brown spots the size of raisins, and her shiny nails looked like the wings of red beetles. She teased students and often made comments that made the class laugh. I laughed too, even though sometimes I did not understand her jokes.

No one laughed at her homework assignments, though. Every week she gave us vocabulary and spelling lists and a poem to memorize. I wrote the poems on notecards and attached them to the broom handle or placed them in my shirt pocket and memorized them as I cleaned the offices after school. I did the same thing with spelling and vocabulary words. I had a harder time with reading and writing. I was a slow reader and often had to read each assignment twice. At times my mind wondered off as I worried about Papá. When we discussed the readings in class, I was surprised to find out that I had not really understood what I read.

Writing was even more difficult for me. Miss Bell asked us to write short compositions analyzing short stories we read for class. I was happy whenever I understood the plot and summarized it, but this was not good enough. "Don't tell me the story," she would say, smiling. "I know it. I want you to analyze it." I thought I knew what she meant, so in my next composition I wrote about the lesson I learned from reading the story. I hoped this was what she wanted. The stories I had heard from Papá and Mamá, Tío Mauricio, and other migrant workers all had a lesson in them about right and wrong, like "La Llorona," "The Boy and His Grandfather," or "The Three Brothers."

When Miss Bell returned our compositions, I fixed my eyes on the stack of papers as she walked around the aisles passing them out, trying to spot mine. The one with the most writing in red was sure to be mine. My papers always came back looking as though she had poured red ink on them. My heart pounded faster with each step she took toward me. She grinned as she handed me my paper. I quickly grabbed it. It had fewer corrections than my previous papers, but the grade was only a disappointing C. I stuck it in my binder, and for the rest of the class I had a hard time concentrating. During study hall, I took out the paper. She had written "Good progress" at the bottom of it. I felt better. I then went over the corrections carefully to make sure I understood them. I did not want to make the same mistakes in my next writing assignment, which Miss Bell announced the following day.

"Our next unit is on autobiography, the history of a

person's life written or told by that person," she explained. "So for your next composition, I want you to write about a personal experience, something that happened to you." I liked the assignment, but it was harder than I expected. I thought of writing about being deported, but I did not want my teacher to know that my family had crossed the border illegally and that I was born in Mexico.

An idea finally came to me late that evening. As I was sitting at the kitchen table trying to figure out what to write, Trampita entered the room, pulling up his white shorts. "What are you doing up?" I asked.

"I am getting a glass of water," he responded, half asleep. His small body cast a thin shadow on the wall. We called him "Trampita," "little tramp," because Mamá had dressed him in baby clothes we found in the city dump. As he passed me on his way back to bed, I noticed his bulging navel, the size of an egg, that had ruptured when he was a few months old.

We had been living in a farm labor camp in Santa Rosa. It was winter. Papá and Mamá worked at an apple cannery at night and left Roberto to take care of Trampita and me while they were gone. One evening, before leaving for work, Mamá prepared the milk bottle for Trampita and laid him on a wide mattress that was on the dirt floor. After my parents left, Roberto and I sat on the mattress and told ghost stories until we got sleepy. We said our prayers and went to bed next to Trampita. We kept our clothes on because it was freezing cold. At dawn, we woke up, frightened by our parents' screams. "Where's Trampita?" Mamá cried out. "Where is he?" Papá shouted. They had terror in their eyes when they saw Trampita was gone.

"I don't know, Mamá," Roberto stuttered, shivering from the cold. Papá noticed an opening at the foot of the tent near the mattress. He rushed out. Seconds later he returned with Trampita in his arms. My baby brother was stiff and purple.

I decided to write about that experience. I wrote three drafts, making sure I did not make any mistakes. I turned it in feeling confident. When I got my paper back, I was disappointed to see the red marks again. I had made a few errors. I felt worse when I read Miss Bell's note at the bottom of the paper, asking me to see her after class. *She must be pretty upset with the mistakes I made*, I thought. I half listened to what she said during the rest of class. When class was over, I waited until everyone had left the room before I approached her, folding the paper in half to hide the red marks.

"Is what you wrote a true story?" Miss Bell asked.

"Yes," I answered, feeling anxious.

"I thought so," she said, smiling. "It's a very moving story. Did your brother die?"

"Oh, no!" I exclaimed. "He almost did, but God saved him. He rolled off the mattress, landed outside the tent, and cried so much that he hurt his navel."

"His hernia must have really hurt," she said thoughtfully. "I am sorry." She looked away and cleared her throat. "Now, let's look at your paper." I handed it to her, lowering my head. "You're making a lot of progress," she said. "Your writing shows promise. If you're able to overcome the difficulties like the one you describe in your paper and you continue working as hard as you have, you're going to succeed." She gave me back the paper and added, "Here, take it home, make the corrections, and turn it in to me tomorrow after class."

"I will. Thank you, Miss Bell." I floated out of the room, thinking about how lucky I was to be in her class. She reminded me of Mr. Lema, my sixth-grade teacher, who had helped me with English during the lunch hour.

That evening when I got home I worked on the paper. I looked at the mistakes I had made and corrected them, following Miss Bell's suggestions. As I retyped it on the kitchen table, Mamá came over and sat next to me. "It's late, Panchito," she said softly. "Time for bed."

"I am almost finished."

"What are you working on, *mijo?*"

"It's a paper I wrote for my English class on Trampita. My teacher liked it," I said proudly.

"On Trampita!" she exclaimed.

She got up and stood behind me. She placed her hands on my shoulders and asked me to read it. When I finished, I felt her tears on the back of my neck.

The next day after class I turned in my revised paper to Miss Bell. She glanced at it, placed it on a pile of papers on her desk, and picked up a book. "Have you read *The Grapes of Wrath?*" she asked. "It's a wonderful novel by John Steinbeck."

"No," I said, wondering what the word *wrath* meant.

"I'd like for you to read it." She handed it to me. "I think you'll enjoy it. You can read it for your book report."

When am I going to find time to read such a thick book? I thought, running my fingers along its spine. I was planning to read a smaller book for my report. Miss Bell must have noticed the pain in my face because she added, "And you'll get extra credit because it's a long book." I felt better.

"Thanks!" I said. "It'll give me a chance to improve my grade." Her gentle smile reminded me of Mamá and the blessing she gave every morning when I left the house.

After my last class, I picked up the books and binders I needed from my locker and walked to the public library to study before going to work at five o'clock. I double-checked to make sure I had the novel with me. On the way, I kept thinking about how I was going to get through such a long book. I felt its weight on my shoulders and the back of my neck. I quickened my pace, passing students left and right. The honking of car horns from students cruising by sounded far away. I rushed into the library and went straight to my table in the left back corner, away from the main desk. I piled my books and binders on the table.

I took a deep breath, picked up the novel, and placed it in front of me. I grabbed my worn-out pocket dictionary from the stack and set it next to it. I muttered the title, *"The Grapes of Wrath."* The word *grapes* reminded me of working in the vineyards for Mr. Sullivan in Fresno. I looked up the word *wrath* and thought of the anger I felt when I lost my blue notepad, my *librito*, in a fire in Orosi. I began reading. It was difficult; I had to look up many words, but I kept on reading. I wanted to learn more about the Joad family, who had to leave their home in Oklahoma to look for work and a better life in California. I lost track of time. Before I knew it, five o'clock had passed. I was late for work.

When I got home that evening, I continued reading until one o'clock in the morning. That night I dreamed that my family was packing to move to Fresno to pick grapes. "We don't have to move anymore! I have to go to school!" I kept yelling, but Papá and Mamá could not hear me. I woke up exhausted.

Saturday night I skipped the school dance and stayed home to read more of the novel. I kept struggling with the reading, but I could not put it down. I finally understood what Miss Bell meant when she told me to read for enjoyment. I could relate to what I was reading. The Joad family was poor and traveled from place to place in an old jalopy, looking for work. They picked grapes and cotton and lived in labor camps similar to the ones we lived in, like Tent City in Santa Maria. Ma Joad was like Mamá and Pa Joad was a lot like Papá. Even though they were not Mexican and spoke only English, they had many of the same experiences as my family. I felt for them. I got angry with the growers who mistreated them and was glad when Tom Joad protested and fought for their rights. He reminded of my friend Don Gabriel, the *bracero* who stood up to Díaz, the labor contractor, who tried to force Don Gabriel to pull a plow like an ox.

After I finished reading the novel, I could not get it out of my mind. I thought about it for days, even after I had turned in the book report to Miss Bell. She must have liked what I wrote, because she gave me a good grade. My success made me happy, but, this time, the grade seemed less important than what I had learned from reading the book.

Broken Heart

I did not have a lot of free time to make close friends and do things with them on weekends. Papá allowed us to go out only once a week, and we had to be home by midnight. I did meet many nice classmates at school, and some of us hung around together at lunchtime in the cafeteria. Most of them bought their lunch, but I always brought mine from home. I asked Mamá not to make *taquitos* for my lunch, because a few guys made fun of me when they saw me eat them. They called me "chile stomper" or "tamale wrapper." I pretended not to get upset. I knew that if they saw me get mad, they would make fun of me even more. So Mamá made baloney sandwiches instead. I ate jalapeño chiles with my sandwiches to give them flavor.

I also made friends, many of them girls, at school dances, which took place after football or basketball games. Because we had to work, Roberto and I usually skipped the games on Friday nights and went only to the dances. They were held in the school cafeteria, and like the Vets dances, the girls stood on one side and the boys on the other. I thought it was strange that some boys drank to get the courage to ask girls to dance. I spent more time on the girls' side, dancing one song after another. The faster the song, the more I liked it. Listening to music and dancing made me forget my troubles.

At one of the dances, I saw Roberto standing on the side, next to a girl who was slightly taller than he was. I did not think anything about it. The room was warm and stuffy, so I walked out to cool off and to get a drink of water. When I returned, my brother was dancing a slow dance with the same girl. I watched him as they danced past me. He caught my eye and moved his cheek away from hers. As they swirled around, I saw that he had his eyes closed. At the end of the song, they strolled across the floor, holding hands, and stood on the side, away from the crowd. I did not want to lose sight of them, so during the next fast song, I purposely moved closer to them, swung around, and bumped into Roberto. "Sorry!" I said. He gave me an annoyed look. The girl I was dancing with did too. As the song was about to end, I quickly walked my dance partner back to the girls' side, thanked her, and raced back to the boys' side, where Roberto and the girl were standing, holding hands. "What do you think you're doing, Panchito?" he whispered, placing his left hand on my left shoulder and digging in his fingers. His large hand felt like a vise.

"Nothing," I said, wincing. "I just lost my balance." Roberto sneered at me. The girl stood behind him, looking around the room, pretending not to pay attention to us. She was slender and had short brown hair, large, droopy brown eyes, a small mouth, and thin lips.

"Well?" I said, gesturing to him to introduce me. Roberto let go of the girl's hand and moved to her side.

"Susan, this is my brother."

"Hi," she said softly.

"You and my brother are good dancers," I said. She smiled and blushed.

Roberto continued dancing with her until we had to leave. The next day I saw them together at school between classes. On our way home from work he told me that he had asked her out to the movies for next Saturday. "That means you won't be going to the dance Saturday?" I was disappointed. Roberto and I did everything together. I did not like the idea of being apart.

"Don't worry, Panchito. I can drop you off at the dance before I go to the movies."

"Wouldn't you rather go dancing?" I insisted.

"No! I am going to the movies with Susan," he said sharply.

I was so upset with my brother that I decided not to go

out at all. I stayed home that Saturday night and tried to study, but I did not get much work done.

Roberto was happy all day at work on Sunday. He whistled and sang while we cleaned offices. "You must've had a good time last night," I said, still feeling hurt because he did not go to the dance.

"I did. And I think I am in love!" he exclaimed.

"Sure, after one date! Are you crazy?"

"I know it's weird," he said, "but I have this strange feeling; it's hard to explain." He placed his right hand on his chest and added, "It's like nothing I felt before. I can't stop thinking about her!"

I liked seeing my brother happy, but I was upset that we were not going to dances together anymore.

Roberto continued going out with Susan once a week. Eventually he asked her to go steady. She wore his jacket at school as a sign that she was his girl. But it did not last.

One rainy Monday evening when Roberto came to pick me up from work, he looked weary and sad. "What's wrong?" I asked as we drove home.

"Susan's parents don't want her to go out with me anymore," he said, teary-eyed.

"Why?" I asked, putting my arm around him.

"Because I am Mexican," he said, raising his voice and hitting the steering wheel with both hands.

"Because you're Mexican! What do you mean?"

Roberto took a deep breath and explained. "Well,

Susan invited me to dinner at her house last Saturday. She said her parents wanted to get to know me. I was very nervous, but once we sat at the table and started talking, I felt better. During the conversation her father asked me what my nationality was."

"Why did he ask you?" I said, recalling the time I met Peggy's parents.

"He wanted to know where the name *Jiménez* came from. I told him."

"You didn't tell him . . ."

"No, I didn't tell him I was born in Mexico," he said, anticipating my question. "But when I said I was Mexican there was dead silence. After a while we continued talking, but they seemed uncomfortable and less friendly. I thought it was strange, but I didn't think much about it until Susan told me today at school. She couldn't stop crying. I felt terrible." Roberto choked up. "Her father even promised to buy her a car if she stopped seeing me. Can you believe it?"

Then, like a flash, it became clear why Peggy stopped seeing me. I felt angry and insulted, but most of all, confused. I could not understand why anyone would not like us because we were Mexican. Mamá told us everyone was equal in the eyes of God and Papá told us we should respect everyone.

"What are you going to do?" I asked after a long pause.

"She still wants to go out with me, but doesn't want

her parents to know," he responded. "I don't feel right doing that."

Roberto went out with Susan a few more times, but it was not the same. My brother picked her up at her friend's house, where she told her parents she was spending the night. He did not like her to be sneaking out, and when her father found out she had been lying he did not allow her to go out at all. Eventually she started seeing some-one else. My brother stopped dating for a long time.

Behind the Wheel

The summer at the end of my sophomore year, Roberto taught me how to drive the Santa Maria Window Cleaners van on weekends. I started my lessons in the parking lot behind the gas company. The van and I did not get along. Every time I got behind the wheel, it jerked and sputtered. When I applied the brakes, which I did every few feet, brooms and mops ended up in the front seat. My brother's patience got shorter and his prayers got longer as I drove around in circles as if I were on a merry-go-round. I perfected my right turns, but the rest of my driving skills needed a lot of work. When I finally took the exam for my driver's license, I got a hundred percent on the written section but barely passed the driving test.

Once I got my driver's license, I was anxious to drive any car other than our DeSoto. The car had been in a wreck. The window on the driver's side did not close all the way. The front left door was smashed in and did not close either, so we secured it with a rope. I begged Roberto like a child to let me drive his Buick. He often gave in, but one time when he did not, I got mad and yelled at him. Papá heard me. "What's the matter with you, Panchito?" he said angrily. "You can't yell at Roberto. He's your older brother. Apologize."

"I am sorry," I said, lowering my head.

"Why don't you give him the keys to the DeSoto, *viejo?*" Mamá said to Papá.

"You mean the DeSoto *viejo*," Trampita said.

"It's not that old," Papá said. "It still runs."

"Like a turtle," Trampita responded, laughing. "It's Panchito's speed."

Knowing that Trampita and Torito hid in the back seat so their friends would not see them in the DeSoto when Mamá drove them to school every time they missed the bus, I said, "I'll drive you to school in it tomorrow." Trampita made a face. I knew he liked to drive in my brother's car. Sometimes he and Torito would get up extra early to get a ride to school in the Buick with Roberto and me.

But no one liked the Buick as much as Roberto. It was his pride and joy. He took care of it as though it were part of him. He washed and polished it once a week and dusted it every day with a rag he kept underneath the front seat. The interior was spotless. His high school friend who

worked at an upholstery shop tucked and rolled the dashboard in exchange for a record player cabinet my brother
made in wood shop. On the side of both fenders, Roberto
installed six-inch chrome pipes in the three portals and
strung tiny white lights underneath the car frame. He
took a broken portable record player that someone had
thrown away, fixed it, placed it on the floor of the front
seat, rewired it, and plugged it in to the cigarette lighter
in the car. He played records on it when the car was
parked. Next to the gas tank door he painted a small
skunk with a sign above it that read LITTLE STINKER. I
tried to convince him not to do it because I thought it
was silly, but he ignored me. "I like it!" he told me proudly. "Besides, it's my car." Papá must have liked it too,
because he did not say anything about it to my brother.

Most of the high school guys who had cars decorated
them. On Saturday nights they cruised up and down
Broadway, showing them off and dragging when the police
were not around. Roberto did not have time to cruise, but
he took pride when people gawked at his car.

My joy of going to school with Roberto in his Buick
and driving home with him after work ended when Mike
Nevel asked me to clean the Western Union every morning before it opened at seven o'clock. I was tempted to
say no because I had to get up extra early and drive the
DeSoto, but Papá taught us never to turn down work.
Besides, we needed the extra money. After I cleaned the

Western Union, I would drive to school, taking side streets so that my classmates would not see me. I would park the car several blocks away from school, behind the county fairgrounds, and walk to class.

One day Roberto passed by as I was walking out of the fairgrounds on my way to school. I looked the other way, hoping he did not see me. The next morning he got up at the same time I did. "Why are you getting up so early?" I asked.

"I am helping you clean the Western Union."

"You are!" I exclaimed, smiling ear to ear. "This means..."

"Yes, give Papá the keys to the DeSoto. You won't need them."

After cleaning the Western Union, Roberto and I drove up Broadway to school, just like before. The Little Stinker decal did not bother me as much anymore.

Turning a Page

At the beginning of my junior year, I went to see my counselor, Mr. Kinkade, to go over my class schedule. On my way to his office, I thought about the first day of my freshman year when I met him. This time I felt much more confident. I walked in his office. He was sitting at his desk, talking on the phone. He motioned for me to sit down across from him. He wore the same dark gray suit that he wore two years before. It sagged around his shoulders, and its color matched his hair. The piles of paper on his desk and the top of his file cabinet had grown. I glanced out the window to the left. The garden in the courtyard looked the same as it did my freshman year. He hung up the phone, picked up my file from his desk, and glanced at it. "You did very well last year," he said, "except in driver education. You made the California Scholarship Federation. Congratulations."

"I had trouble parallel parking," I said, feeling embarrassed.

Everyone had told me that driver education was an easy A, but not for me. Every time I got behind the steering wheel I got nervous because I remembered the time our *Carcachita* was hit from behind by a drunk driver in Selma. None of us was hurt, but it scared me. If it had not been for Roberto and those driving lessons in the van behind the gas company, I would have done worse, and I would not have gotten my driver's license.

"Don't worry about it. Just don't park next to my car," Mr. Kinkade said, laughing. "The important thing is that you're on the right track for college," he added.

"I hear college is really hard," I said, remembering how anxious I felt when Mrs. Taylor, my social studies teacher, told the class how difficult college was compared to high school. She reminded us whenever someone grumbled about homework or grades, which was at least once every class. Mr. Kinkade stared at me briefly, then looked out the window.

"It all depends," he said. "If you're well prepared in high school, you shouldn't have trouble in college."

"But what's the difference?" I asked.

"Difference?" he responded, looking puzzled.

"What's the difference between college and high school?"

Mr. Kinkade grinned, took off his glasses, leaned forward, and said, "Rather than my telling you, why don't you visit one of our local colleges and find out for yourself? In a few weeks we're taking California Scholarship Federation students by bus to Cal Poly in San Luis Obispo to visit the campus. I'll sign you up for it."

I was the first one on the bus the day of the field trip to Cal Poly. I sat toward the front with Ernie and Bob, two of my friends whom I had met in the Squires Club. On our way to Cal Poly we talked about classes and the dance coming up that Saturday night. As soon as they began discussing sports, I tuned out. I looked out the window. The highway snaked through green rolling hills past Nipomo, Arroyo Grande, and Pismo Beach until we reached San Luis Obispo. The bus went up a grade, onto the campus, and parked in front of the administration building. A tall, thin young man greeted us and gave us a walking tour, pointing out buildings and explaining different programs. He talked about majors, semesters, units, and many other things I did not understand. *Maybe this is what my teacher meant when she said college was difficult,* I thought. Surrounded by eucalyptus and pepper trees, the buildings were far apart and scattered throughout the campus. The air smelled fresh and sweet. I kept eyeing students who walked by, trying to see if they looked smart. They appeared to be like many of the older students at

Santa Maria High School, but none looked like my friends from Bonetti Ranch or friends I made in other labor camps, and that made me feel uncomfortable.

In the afternoon we visited one of the dormitories that was far away from the administration building. It was a long concrete building with windows in every room. It looked like a fancy army barrack. We went into the lounge to look around and rest for a few minutes. I saw a student sitting on a light brown couch, reading. He had on a gray sweatshirt that read CAL POLY. I wondered if he felt lonely, like Roberto and I did when we lived alone. The student seemed annoyed by the noise we were making. He looked up, made a bad face, and left in a hurry, leaving one of his books behind on the couch. He was gone before I had a chance to tell him. I assumed it was a college book and wondered if I would be able to read it. Just as I was about to move toward the couch, I heard the guide say, "Time to head back." Everyone followed him out the door, but I stayed behind and waited until everyone had left before picking it up. It was an American history textbook. I looked at the table of contents, turned the page, and started reading. "I can read this!" I exclaimed under my breath. *Maybe college isn't as hard as my teacher said it is*, I thought. That evening at work I thought about our visit to Cal Poly. I imagined myself in college and living in the dorm, away from home. I felt excited and sad at the same time.

Los Santitos

I liked being at school, and I got involved in school activities whenever I could. I joined the Squires Club, and our main duties were to keep order in the lunch line and stop students from littering. I missed the initiation dinner, which was held on a Thursday evening, because I had to work.

I also became a member of the Spanish Club. In late fall of my junior year, my study hall teacher announced that a meeting was being held after school for students interested in joining the club. I decided to attend and learn more about it. Instead of going straight to the public library to do my math homework as I usually did, I went to the meeting, which was held in one of the classrooms in the old part of the school, next to the tennis courts. Few students were there. Mr. Osterveen, one of the Spanish teachers, ran the meeting. He was a short, stocky man with a large head and receding hairline. He had a long chin and a thin, black mustache, just like Papá's. As he talked about Mexico, his small, dark eyes lit up like a cat's when it saw a mouse. He said he was from New York but had lived and studied in Mexico City, where he met his wife, who was from Oaxaca. I had heard of Mexico City but not of Oaxaca and I wondered if those places were like El Rancho Blanco or Guadalajara. He rested his right foot on one of the desks in the front row, and each time he got excited, he pushed up, making himself look taller. I felt right at home when he spoke Spanish. I signed up to be a member right there and then. Mr. Osterveen suggested a second meeting to elect officers and to come up with a new name for the club. We all agreed to meet again a few weeks later.

When I got home that evening after work I told my family about the club and Mr. Osterveen. "And he's a teacher?" Papá asked. I was surprised to see him so interested. He usually never asked anything about school.

"Yes, he speaks Spanish just like us," I said enthusiastically.

"Is he from Jalisco?"

"No, but he lived in Mexico for many years."

Papá smiled and nodded his head. I then asked my family to help me think of names for the club.

"How about 'The Little Stinkers'?" Trampita said,

chuckling. Roberto gave Trampita a slight punch on the shoulder and laughed.

"You're the stinker," he said. "That's why we call you Trampita."

"Come on, get serious," I said. "How about 'The Spanish Club Saints'?"

"*Los Santitos*," Mamá uttered, "*Los Santitos*, like all our children."

"*Santitos!*" Papá exclaimed. "How about *Los Diablitos* . . ."

"I like *Los Santitos*," I said. "It fits with the Santa Maria Saints."

At the next meeting of the Spanish Club I proposed the name *Los Santitos*. Everyone voted in favor of it. We then elected officers. I was elected president, Abie Gonzales, vice president, Charlotte Woodward, secretary, and Marjorie Ito, coordinator of social events. Our first order of business was to think of an activity for the club. Marjorie suggested having a Thanksgiving fiesta. I liked the idea of celebrating Thanksgiving. It was my favorite holiday because when we picked cotton in Corcoran I started school around that time every year. We all went along with her idea, except Mr. Osterveen. He reminded us that Thanksgiving was only a few days away. "You don't have time to organize a party around Thanksgiving," he said, "but you could for Christmas."

I thought about Christmas and felt sad, recalling living

in tent labor camps in Corcoran during that holiday and seeing families struggling to make ends meet.

"What do you think?" Abie said, poking me in the back.

"About Christmas? Well ..." I hesitated. I then remembered the Christmas when Papá gave Mamá an embroidered handkerchief he had bought from a young couple who needed money to buy food. "What about collecting food for poor families?" I finally said.

"A Christmas food drive. That's a great idea!" Mr. Osterveen said. Abie and Majorie agreed. "I'll ask teachers to announce it in study hall. Students can drop off food cans in the cafeteria and we'll have the Salvation Army deliver it to needy families," Mr. Osterveen added.

We left the meeting and agreed to meet once again before the Christmas break to make sure everything was in order. Every day the number of food bags increased, and by the end of the second week in December we had collected forty-one bags. On the last day of school before Christmas break, Captain Tracy from the Salvation Army came to collect the food. He thanked *Los Santitos* and gave us a certificate of appreciation for "rendering eminent and memorable service to the Santa Maria community by helping the Salvation Army to give a happy Christmas."

That evening after I finished cleaning the gas company I waited for Roberto to pick me up. I was excited because he was bringing home a Christmas tree. Ever since Roberto started working at Main Street Elementary School, Mr. Sims told him that he could take the school Christmas tree home on the day the school closed for the holidays. I sat down in the main office of the gas company and admired the large, cheerful Santa Claus painted on the front window and the tall Christmas tree in the middle of the office, with its tiny white lights blinking off and on like stars in the heavens. I saw my brother drive up. I quickly locked the office and rushed to the parking lot to see the tree. It was in the back seat of the car, strewn with tinsel. "It's a beautiful tree," Roberto said. "Wait till you see it standing up." When we got home Trampita, Rorra, Torito, and Rubén dashed out of the house to see it.

"This is a very special Christmas, _mijo_," Mamá said excitedly, clasping her hands. "This afternoon the Salvation Army brought us a huge box full of groceries. God is truly watching over us."

Choosing Sides

I became interested in politics in my U.S. history class during my junior year. Miss Kellog, the teacher, required our class to follow the 1960 presidential campaign. She talked about Vice President Richard Nixon and Senator John F. Kennedy as though she knew them personally. "It's your responsibility as citizens to be informed about what's happening in politics," she said often. "Our democracy depends on it." Few students shared her enthusiasm. I paid close attention because I was interested and because I wanted Miss Kellog and my classmates to think I was an American citizen.

One of her class assignments was for us to ask our parents their opinion on politics and the presidential campaign. Papá, who was in one of his bad moods, did not want to talk about it, but Mamá finally convinced him. "I don't know much," Papá said. "I didn't go to school, but

I can tell you that in Mexico the rich have all the power. They choose the president, not the people. They tell us we have a vote, but it means nothing."

"But here it's different," I said. "This is a democracy."

"That's what they say, but I believe the rich rule here too," he said. "And the rich don't care about poor people."

"How do you know?" I asked, forgetting that Papá did not like us to question him. He gave me a stern look.

"Because I've lived many years," he responded in a harsh tone of voice. His lips were thin and pale. "I have seen it with my own eyes," he added. He got up from the table and went into his room and slammed the door. Mamá looked at me and shook her head.

"Do you agree with him?" I asked.

"Not completely," she responded, glancing at Papá's room. "I think he's right about the government in Mexico, but in this country..." She hesitated for a moment and then continued, "I heard on the radio that Kennedy will help poor people."

"So you're in favor of the Democratic Party," I said.

"I am in favor of Kennedy. That's all I know," she said.

If he gets elected, he'll help people like us, I thought. At that moment, I decided to be for Kennedy and the Democratic Party from then on.

The next day in class we continued talking about the two presidential candidates. Some students supported

Nixon, others favored Kennedy. Miss Kellog did not take sides, but I figured she must have preferred Kennedy because her eyes sparkled whenever she talked about him. Besides, I could not imagine her not supporting the candidate who wanted to aid the poor. When I found out that Kennedy came from a wealthy family, I knew for sure that Papá was wrong about rich people, but I never said anything to him. I knew better.

The next class assignment was for us to watch the presidential debates on television, take notes, and discuss them in class. I missed all four of the debates because I had to work. I did not participate in class discussions, but I listened carefully, always rooting for Kennedy.

At the end of the semester, after the elections, we were to turn in a scrapbook with all the articles about the campaign published in the *Santa Maria Times*, the local newspaper. We did not get the paper at home, so at work every day I picked up the discarded newspaper from the day before, took it home, and piled it in the shed next to our barrack. I spent one Sunday evening putting the scrapbook together. I brought out the stack of papers and placed them on the kitchen table. Roberto sat next to me, helping me clip articles. Mamá ironed while she listened to the Spanish radio station. "You have enough paper there to plug every hole in all the barracks in Bonetti Ranch," Mamá said, laughing. I explained what I was doing. "I am glad Kennedy won," she said. "He gives us hope."

"I am too," I said, glancing at her and continuing to work. She smiled and turned off the radio. I reread some of the articles and read others for the first time. "I can't believe this!" I exclaimed as I finished reading an editorial on the results of the presidential election.

"What?" Mamá asked, leaning over the ironing board.

"Did you know that some people didn't vote for Kennedy because he is Catholic?" I said, raising my voice and slamming the paper on the table.

"Why are you surprised?" Roberto said, pushing back his chair and leaning back. "Some people don't like Mexicans and wouldn't vote for them either." I knew he was thinking about Susan.

"But why?" I felt upset and angry. "Papá said we should respect everyone."

"It's true, *mijo*," Mamá said, "but some people are blinded by the devil. He plants evil seeds in their hearts."

Papá appeared in the doorway. "What's all the fuss about?" he said, looking annoyed. He winced as he pulled out a chair and slowly sat next to Roberto.

"Panchito doesn't understand why some people don't like Mexicans," Mamá said, walking over and massaging Papá's shoulders.

"Or Catholics," I quickly added.

"Because people are ignorant," Papá said. "I am proud of being Catholic and Mexican and you must be too."

"I am," Roberto, said, "but some aren't. The janitor at Main Street School who is Mexican told me that Panchito and I could pass for Americans because we're light. 'Don't tell people you're Mexican,' he said. 'You could easily pass for Americans.'"

"*Que lástima*," Mamá said.

"Yes, it's a pity," Roberto agreed.

"I never hide that I am Mexican," I said. "I am proud of it too. Besides, even if I tried to hide it, I couldn't; my accent gives me away. My friends tell me they can cut it with a knife."

"A knife! You need a machete," Roberto said. We all laughed.

It was late in the evening when I finally finished reading and pasting the last article. Everyone had gone to bed. I reread the editorial and thought of Susan and Peggy and became angry again. I felt like shredding it. I closed the scrapbook and went to bed. I had a hard time falling asleep.

Junior Scandals

Many of my classmates knew I was Mexican and those who did not found out when I participated in Junior Scandals, an annual event sponsored by the junior class. Marvin Bell, our junior class president, who sat next to me in Miss Kellog's class, asked me to be part of it that year. "Frankie, how about doing something for Junior Scandals?" he said enthusiastically as we walked into class.

"What is it?" I asked.

"Okay, class, let's get settled," Miss Kellog said, directing her attention to Marvin and me.

"Here, read this," he whispered. He handed me a copy of *The Breeze*, the school newspaper, and pointed to the article on the front page.

I glanced at the article. It read "Junior Scandals Slated for March Showing." I folded it and placed it underneath my desk. At the end of class, Marvin again insisted.

"You gotta help our class, man. Don't chicken out." He gave me a slight shove and added, "I am counting on you."

I read the article during study hall.

> Attention student body! "Tenth Anniversary," this year's Junior Scandals, will be presented Friday, March 4, beginning at 8:00 P.M. in the boys' gym. Pantomimes, dancing, singing, the familiar chorus line, and a boys' fashion show will be a few of the acts. Marvin Bell, junior class president, will preside over the scandals as master of ceremonies. Be sure not to miss this year's presentation of Junior Scandals, as this will be the finest Scandals ever presented.

I looked up the word *scandal* in my dictionary. I did not like the sound of it.

"Why would our class want to put on a shameful show?" I asked Marvin the next day after class.

"It's not shameful," he said. "It's entertaining."

"Like what?" I asked.

"Didn't you read the article? Some of the guys are dressing up as girls and modeling," he said, laughing. "You could join them."

"That's crazy! Why would guys want to dress up as girls?"

"You don't get it, man. It's all for fun."

"Can I do something that's not disrespectful . . . I mean, that's not funny?"

"Sure, you can do whatever you want," he said, giving me an odd look. "Everyone who's participating will meet in the boys' gym next Monday, right after school. Be there or be square!"

Before I got a chance to respond, he said, "See you later, alligator," and rushed off. I had a hard time making up my mind about performing in front of a crowd. What if they made fun of my accent? Then I remembered making a lot of friends in the eighth grade when I sang an Elvis Presley song. I wanted to be a part of my class, so I decided to participate. Trampita offered to help me clean the gas company on Friday so that I could finish work in time to make the performance at eight o'clock. Now I had to think of a skit. I did not have much time. By Sunday early evening I was still struggling for an idea. I asked Roberto to help me.

"Why don't you do Elvis Presley, like in El Camino?" he said.

Just as Roberto said Elvis Presley, Papá walked in. He had been cutting wood for Bonetti on a power saw in the shed. "Who's El Vez?" he asked, dusting off his pants. "I never heard of him.

"He's an American singer."

"*Que* El Vez *ni que* El Vez. Jorge Negrete!" he said sharply, stating his preference for the Mexican star. He turned on the radio and searched for a Mexican station. "Mi Tierra" by Pedro Infante came on. As a child I loved listening to him and Jorge Negrete. Papá and Roberto often whistled their songs when we worked in the fields. Suddenly a strange and strong emotion took over me: I felt homesick. Roberto must have read my mind because he said, "Why don't you sing a Mexican song?"

"I was thinking the same thing. What song should I sing?"

"'Cielito Lindo,'" Roberto said. "You've always liked that song."

"That's it," I said. "I know it by heart and I don't have to worry about my accent!" Papá's eyes watered. He smiled and lowered the volume on the radio. All three of us sat at the kitchen table in silence and listened to music.

On Monday after school I headed for the gym. Many of my classmates were already there checking in. Marvin announced that Mr. Ward Kinkade, my counselor, and Mr. Wesley Hodges, my P.E. coach, would be supervising the performance, and Bobbie Sue Winters and Glenna Burns were coordinating the event.

"Okay, you guys, break up into groups according to your skits and tell us what your skit is going to be," Bobbie Sue shouted. Her high-pitched voice echoed throughout the gym. Mr. Kinkade and Mr. Hodges leaned against the wall, arms folded and whispering to each other. The large crowd separated into small groups. I stood alone underneath the basketball hoop, listening and waiting for my turn.

Greg Kudron, who was closest to Bobbie Sue, reported first. "We're going to dress up as girls and model," he said, pointing behind him to a large group of guys who wore football jerseys. The gym filled with laughter. I felt uneasy. Once the noise faded, Judy Treankler, one of the most popular girls in our class, stepped forward and introduced her skit.

"We're the chorus line," she said, pushing her hair back with her right hand. The nine girls in her group kicked up their right legs in unison. The boys gyrated, whistled, and screamed. When I saw Mr. Kinkade and Mr. Hodges laughing, I laughed too.

The different groups and individuals continued to report on their skits one by one. George Harshbarger and his trio and I were the last two. George played the banjo and Jim Hodges and Roger Brown played the guitar. I had seen them perform at several school dances.

"Go ahead, Frankie," George said.

"No, you go next," I responded, feeling tense.

"Thanks," he said. Jim and Roger followed behind him, strumming their guitars. "We're going to sing a few folk songs," he said, picking his banjo.

"Like the Kingston Trio," someone yelled out from the back of the crowd.

"Exactly," George responded.

"You're next, Frankie," Bobbie Sue said.

I stepped forward, took a deep breath, and said, "I am going to sing 'Cielito Lindo,' a Mexican song." I glanced at Mr. Kinkade. He nodded and applauded. I heard a few cheers from the crowd. I felt more at ease.

"Good job. It's going to be the best Junior Scandals ever!" Bobbie Sue said. "Tell your friends to buy tickets. They're now on sale in the student activities room. The price is seventy-five cents for students and one dollar for adults."

"What are you going to do for music?" George asked as we headed out of the gym.

"I haven't figured that out yet," I said.

"Do you play the guitar?"

"No, I wish I did."

"Maybe I can play for you," he said.

"Would you?" I exclaimed. "Do you know 'Cielito Lindo'?" I asked.

"No, but I can come up with the chords if you sing it," he said.

We went in the cafeteria and sat at an empty table. I hummed it while George listened carefully, trying to follow me. We went over it until he could play it all the way through. He gave me some hints on how to project my voice, and before we left, we agreed to meet a few times after school to practice together.

The school gym was packed the night of the event. A

makeshift stage was set up at the south end of the basketball court, closest to the boys' locker room, where we
dressed and waited to perform. The girls got ready in their
locker room, located on the north end. Tension and
excitement filled the air. Some boys buzzed around the
locker room like sleepless flies, banging on the metal
lockers and walls; others shadowboxed. George and his
trio huddled in the corner, tuning their instruments. I
paced the floor holding my wide-brimmed Mexican hat
against my chest to protect it from being crushed. As
the cheers and applause at the end of each act got louder, I became more and more nervous. I was next. "You're
up, Frankie," Marvin shouted. I put on my hat, wiped my
sweaty hands on my pants, and lightly kissed my Saint
Christopher medal. George followed behind me, strumming his guitar. As I walked up to the stage, my legs
wobbled. I grabbed the microphone with both hands and
glanced at the crowd. I was petrified.

"Are you ready?" George said.

I opened my mouth, but no words came out. My mouth
felt as though it was stuffed with cotton. Then I heard
Roberto holler from the back of the bleachers, "*No te
rajes*, Panchito!" As his words of support echoed throughout the gym, Papá's face flashed in my mind. I slowly
released the microphone, took a deep breath, tilted my
hat, and said, "Okay, I am ready." The words to "Cielito
Lindo" flowed like a stream. Halfway through the song,

several people in the audience sang along to the refrain, "*Ay, ay, ay, ay, canta y no llores,*" and at the end they cheered and applauded. George and I bowed and left. Marvin then went to the microphone and asked all of the participants to join him onstage. We all got a standing ovation. After the audience had left, we cleared the stage, played rock 'n' roll, and danced the Chicken, the Mash Potato, the Twist, the Stroll, and many other dances. On the way home that evening and for days after, I kept hearing "Cielito Lindo" in my mind.

Running for Office

As a result of Junior Scandals, Paul Takagi became my new best friend. We met the day after the event, right before lunch. I was in the hallway putting my books in my locker, when he came up to me. He had short, straight, jet-black hair with an elevated wave at the front. His clothes were loose-fitting. "Hi, Frankie. I heard you sing Friday night," he said. "My name is Paul."

"Hi," I responded, picking up my lunch bag and closing the locker.

"'Cielito Lindo' is one of my favorite songs," he said, adjusting his thick, black-rimmed glasses behind his large ears. He pronounced the name in perfect Spanish.

"How do you know it?" I asked.

"My father taught it to me. I can play it on the piano," he said proudly.

"Does your father speak Spanish?"

"Yes, he learned it in Mexico when he was a missionary there. He's now a church minister here in Santa Maria." His playful look and gangly manner reminded me of Miguelito, my friend in elementary school.

"Want to have lunch together?" I asked.

"If you don't mind sharing your lunch with me," he said.

"You can have my hot peppers," I said, laughing.

"Get out of here!" he said, poking me slightly with his long, slender fingers.

Paul and I ate our lunch and talked about everything, as though we had known each other for a long time. When we found out we were taking the same courses, we decided to study together. Every day after school we drove straight to the public library in my 1950 green Ford, which Papá bought from a neighbor after the DeSoto fell apart. We did our chemistry and Algebra II homework. When we disagreed in our answers, Paul was usually right. His mind was as sharp as Papá's. He solved problems and explained them step by step, in simple words. When we worked together I lost track of time. Paul had to remind me that we had to leave a little before five o'clock. I dropped him off at home on my way to work at the gas company.

The day before Easter vacation, Paul and I were having our lunch in the cafeteria when Linda Spain, one of our classmates, walked up to our table and asked us to sign her petition to run for student body secretary. We both signed it.

"Thanks, guys," she said, smiling, and raced to the next table to get more signatures.

"Why don't you run for president?" Paul said, placing his pen back in his shirt pocket.

"Are you serious?" I responded. "I don't have time. Why don't you?"

"I've been thinking of running for student body treasurer," Paul said.

"Good! I'll vote for you," I said enthusiastically. "With your mind for numbers we'll never lose a penny."

"Get out of here!" he responded, laughing. He slid over closer to me and added, "I am serious."

"I am too," I said. "You'll make a great treasurer."

"No, I mean, you should run for office," he insisted.

"I barely have time to do my homework now," I said. "I can't take on more."

"It won't take a lot of time. We'll work together and . . ."

"If elected," I said, interrupting him.

"You're right. I might not get elected," he said, giving me a sad look.

"I don't mean you," I responded. "I was talking about me."

"Don't be such a pessimist," he said.

"A what? I am not a pest," I said. Paul shook his head and smiled.

"Look, you have a good chance of winning. People know you. Junior Scandals made you famous!"

"Get out of here!" I said, imitating him. We both laughed.

Paul glanced at me from the corner of his eye, smirked, and said, "If elected..." He paused, turned around, looked straight in my eyes, and continued, "I mean, *when* elected, we'll have fun. And it'll help us get into college."

"It will?" I asked, perking up.

Paul gave me a puzzled look. When he saw I was serious and waiting for an answer, he said, "Yep, colleges like it when students do extra stuff at school, like running for student body office."

The bell rang. We cleared the table and picked up our books. Before heading for our separate classes, Paul said, "Go get your petition. I want to be the first one to sign it."

"I'll think about it and let you know when we come back from Easter."

During Easter break I did not think about running for student body president. I spent the little free time I had reading Walt Whitman's *Leaves of Grass* and memorizing a poem for English and keeping up with current events by reading the daily newspaper for my history class. I wrote the poem on an index card and memorized

it while I cleaned the gas company. After I finished cleaning, I quickly scanned the newspaper. An article on sit-in
demonstrations in the South caught my attention. I read
about racial segregation and black students fighting for
equal rights. I heard more about it on the car radio on the
way home that evening. I felt angry that blacks were not
allowed to sit with whites in bus stations. During Easter
Sunday Mass, I kept thinking about it. *How can this be
happening if we're all equal in the eyes of God?*

On Monday morning, the day after Easter, I felt very
tired. My shoulders ached. I finished cleaning the Western
Union and headed for school. As I approached the school
grounds, I remembered my promise to Paul. I had to make
a decision. I parked the car and walked across the campus
to my P.E. class. On the way I ran into Manuelito Martínez,
whose family worked in the fields and lived in Bonetti
Ranch. We had known each other since we were eight
years old. "Hey, Panchito," he said. "I hear you're running
for student body president. That's cool."

"Who told you?"

"*Tu amiguito* Paul, a few minutes ago," he responded.
"*Órale*, that's cool, man."

"*Gracias*, Manuelito. I am thinking about it," I
responded, slightly upset with Paul.

"Don't think about it, man. Do it. Everyone in Bonetti
Ranch will be proud."

I knew what Manuelito meant. Like my family, most

residents of Bonetti Ranch were Mexican or Mexican American field laborers. We lived near Santa Maria but we were far apart from it.

During P.E. the coach asked us to run laps around the track. As I ran I thought about Manuelito and the experiences I shared with him and others in Bonetti Ranch; I thought about racial segregation in the South and about Paul's remark about college. I slowed down to catch my breath and then continued running, cutting through the thick, cool morning fog. At the end of the period, I quickly took a shower, got dressed, and rushed to the main office to pick up a petition. At lunchtime, Paul asked me if I had made a decision.

"I forgot all about it," I said, trying to keep a straight face.

"Get out of here!" he exclaimed. "You're kidding, right?"

"No, I am not," I said. "If I run and win, I'd have to study more in the evenings after work, sleep less, and skip some school dances."

Paul's smile disappeared. He nodded and said, "I understand, man." He pulled out a piece of paper from his worn-out binder. "Here's my petition. I want you to be the first one to sign it."

"I won't sign it," I said.

"Get out of here!" Paul said, taking off his glasses and staring at me.

"Not unless you sign mine," I said, pulling out my petition and handing it to him.

"You had me going!" Paul cried out. "You'll make a good politician." We laughed, shook hands, and signed each other's petitions.

During the next few days Paul and I drove to his church after school to study and to work on making posters for our campaigns. The church was in the north part of town. It was a large, wooden rectangular building with high ceilings and small, square windows on the sides. The front was simple. It had a lectern in the middle and a piano in the right-hand corner. It had neither statues of saints or Christ nor an image of the *Virgen de Guadalupe*, like the church that my family and I attended when we could. We did our homework in Paul's father's office, which was a small private room in the back of the building. We worked on algebra until four o'clock and then made posters for about half an hour, using school supplies from the church. Before I left for work, we took a break. Paul played the piano while I ate a slice of rhubarb pie, which his mother made and left at the church for us every day. After I left for work, Paul went back to school to put up posters for both of us. I got home much later than usual during that week because I had to make up for lost time. I stayed at the gas company after work until I finished my homework. Papá got angry even though I explained to him why I was late. Mamá understood and calmed him down every time.

I was upset when I found out I was running against George Harshbarger for president. He had helped me with Junior Scandals, and now I was his rival. I sought him out and told him how I felt. "Don't be silly," he said. "May the best man win."

On the day before the elections, George and I had to give speeches before a school assembly. In the past, candidates for student body president had presented humorous skits before their speech. One rode into the gym on a small tricycle, followed by his friends, who dressed as hillbillies. His opponent rode a mule. I did not feel comfortable putting on a funny skit, so I asked Paul if he would play the piano. He agreed. At the assembly, George was introduced first. He sang with his trio and gave his speech. I was so nervous I did not pay attention to what he said. I went next. My heart raced and my legs trembled as I gave the shortest talk in the history of Santa Maria High School. "I am a man of few words," I said. "Please vote for me." I paused for a few seconds. Then borrowing from the school's motto, "Enter to Learn, Go Forth to Serve," I added: "If you elect me I will go forth to serve all of you." I gave Paul the sign and he played the first parts of "Cielito Lindo" and "When the Saints Go Marching In," the school's theme song. The audience broke out in applause. I sighed with relief. I was glad the assembly was over.

Students voted all day Friday and that afternoon the results came in: Paul and I had won. Ernie DeGasparis, another friend of ours, was elected vice president and Linda Spain, secretary. We were so excited that instead of going to the public library after school to study, we drove straight to Leo's Drive-in on North Broadway to celebrate. Paul and I sat in the car, drinking Coke and talking about the campaign, the assembly, and the election. We relived and savored every moment. I then dropped Paul at his church and I sped home to tell my parents before going to work. I felt like flying. I turned into Bonetti Ranch and passed Manuelito, who was just getting home from school. He yelled out, "Way to go, Panchito!" I waved and smiled proudly. As soon as I drove by Joe and Espy's house, I saw Torito rush out their door. He was crying hysterically.

"What's wrong?" I asked, hugging him. "Why aren't you home?"

"Papá ... Papá hurt himself," he said, shaking and out of breath.

"How? Where is he?" I exclaimed, terrified.

"He cut his hand real bad. Roberto and Mamá took him to the hospital and left me with Joe and Espy." He took a deep breath. "It's my fault," he continued, sobbing.

"What do you mean?"

"I was helping him cut wood for Bonetti on the power saw in the shed. I picked up a board to put it on the saw.

Papá thought my hand was going to touch the blade, so he pushed it away and caught his on the saw." He started crying again.

"It wasn't your fault; it was an accident," I said, trying to calm him down. We got in the car and rushed to Santa Maria County Hospital, which was a few blocks from the high school. We checked in at the front desk and went to his room. Papá lay in bed, white as the sheets. His right hand was bandaged. Mamá sat on his left side, stroking his gray hair and crying. The front of her yellow sweater was stained with blood. Roberto, Trampita, Rorra, and Rubén stood around the bed, heads down and sobbing.

"He cut off his finger," Mamá said, quivering.

My throat tightened like a knot. I approached the bed and kissed Papá on the forehead. "I am sorry, Papá," I said.

He looked up at me and grinned. "I've lost part of my body, *mijo*," he said. "It doesn't matter; it's old and useless." His voice was weak.

"Don't talk like that," Mamá said. "You know that isn't so."

Papá glanced at her and smiled. He then turned to me and asked, "How are you, *mijo*?"

I wiped my eyes with the back of my hand and responded, "I am fine, Papá." Trying to cheer him up, I added, "I got good news, Papá. I was elected student body president and my friend was elected treasurer."

"That's good, *mijo*," Mamá said. Roberto, Trampita, and Torito congratulated me.

"I don't know what it all means," Papá said with a blank look on his face, "but I am happy for you."

I left the hospital and went to work that evening feeling full of both joy and sorrow. By the time I finished cleaning the gas company, I was emotionally exhausted. I felt like a bird caught in a storm.

A New Life

The day Roberto brought his girlfriend Darlene home to meet my parents, I knew he was serious. He had been dating her for over a year but had not brought her home before. My parents somehow knew Roberto had been going out with the same girl on a regular basis, but they never talked about it. This was normal. We never talked seriously about girls and sex at home. But my brother and I always shared our feelings. He told me about her the day after their first date. We were cleaning A. J. Diany, a construction office, and he was whistling and singing like a canary. *"Qué te pasa?"* I asked. "Did you eat birdseed?"

"Darlene is beautiful," he responded, swirling the mop like a dance partner. "Wait till you meet her. She's smart and looks like Elizabeth Taylor." He glowed as he talked about her. I thought he was exaggerating, until I met her.

She did look like Elizabeth Taylor. She had large green eyes, olive skin, and long, jet-black hair combed back in a ponytail. I knew they really loved each other because they continued to date even though her stepfather did not like Mexicans. He used to call Roberto "pepper gut" behind my brother's back just to upset Darlene. He tried to discourage Roberto from dating her by insisting that she be home by midnight. My brother never told her stepfather how happy this made him. He brought Darlene home by eleven-thirty because he had to be home by midnight too.

My brother's face was white as a ghost's and his thick lower lip quivered as he introduced her to our family. Papá and Mamá shook her hand and bowed. Papá signaled to my smaller brothers and sister to leave. They excused themselves and went outside to play. Roberto and Darlene sat across the kitchen table from Mamá, Papá, and me. "Se parece a Dolores del Río," Papá said. Darlene smiled nervously and glanced at Roberto.

"Papá says you look like Dolores del Río."

"She is a pretty Mexican movie star," Mamá said, noticing Darlene's puzzled look.

"Thank you," Darlene said, turning red and looking down.

Papá folded his hands on the table and stared at Roberto, waiting for my brother to break the long silence. Roberto glanced at Darlene, looked up at me, swallowed, and said, "Papá, Darlene and I are getting engaged and we want your blessing."

The words shot out like bullets. I was sure he had re-hearsed them many times. Papá and Mamá looked at each other in surprise. Papá cleared his throat, ready to respond, but Mamá quickly placed her hand on Papá's right hand and burst out, "Of course you have our blessing."

Papá bit his lower lip and nodded in approval. Roberto sighed in relief and smiled. Darlene understood the answer.

My whole family, especially Mamá, got excited when-ever Roberto brought Darlene home to visit. Even Papá, whose moods continued to get darker every day, cheered up when she came. Her visits were like a tonic for him.

At the beginning of the summer before my senior year, Roberto and Darlene got married with her mother's approval but against her stepfather's wishes. My family was happy for them, though worried about how we were going to make ends meet. My brother was concerned too, so he got an extra janitorial job to help us out, but he could not continue beyond the first month. He needed the extra money to attend night classes at Hancock Community College and to pay the medical bills for Darlene, who was expecting a baby. He took a wood shop class to build needed furniture for their one-room apart-ment. Darlene also worked part-time washing dishes at St. Mary's Hospital.

Without Roberto's help, my family struggled even more to make ends meet. Papá became more depressed and often went into the shed, staying there for hours, like a prisoner in a cell. Mamá tried to comfort him. "God will provide; you'll see, *viejo*," she would say. She prayed in front of the faded picture of the *Virgen de Guadalupe*, which hung above their bed. I worried too and began to get headaches. "You're just like your Papá, always worrying," Mamá said when she saw me taking aspirin every morning. "I am sure we'll make it." She was right. Torito and Trampita got jobs picking strawberries for Ito; she took care of babies of working families living in Bonetti Ranch and did ironing for them; I increased my hours at Santa Maria Window Cleaners, working from six in the morning until midnight. In the early morning I cleaned the Western Union and Betty's Fabrics. During the rest of the day I helped Mike Nevel clean houses— doing windows, washing walls, stripping and waxing floors. In the early evenings I did my regular chores at the gas company and late evenings I worked with Mike cleaning the Standard Oil Company, which was located on the outskirts of Santa Maria.

Every day that went by, I felt more and more worn-out. One night while I was cleaning the Standard Oil Company, I felt completely exhausted. I had a hard time keeping my eyes open. I went in the men's bathroom and splashed cold water on my face and arms. I looked in the mirror. My face was haggard and full of blemishes. I had dark circles under my eyes. My pants felt loose around the waist, so I tightened the belt another notch. My reflection reminded me of Papá. I understood for the first time how he must have felt in his darkest moods. I dropped to my knees, buried my face in my hands, and cried.

A Test of Faith

Monday morning, the first day of school my senior year, I could not get out of bed. I had no energy and every joint in my body ached. For a moment I thought I was still asleep because I often dreamed that my legs were too heavy to move. I cried out for help. Mamá rushed in, wiping her hands on her apron, which was covered with white flour.

"Something is wrong with me," I said, trying to hold back my tears. "My whole body aches."

"Calm down, *mijo*," Mamá said. *"Es una pesadilla."*

"No, it's not a nightmare, Mamá," I responded. "Everything hurts!" Mamá sat at the edge of the bed and gently placed her hand on my forehead.

"You don't have a fever," she said. "Let me feel your stomach."

"It's not my stomach," I said. "It's my joints; they hurt when I move."

"When you were little, the skin on your stomach peeled off like it had been burned. You looked like a skinned rabbit," she said worriedly. "I want to make sure it's not that again." She pulled back the blanket and lifted my T-shirt. "No, it's not, thank God," she added, sighing in relief. Papá walked in, holding on to the door frame. His sunken eyes were bloodshot and his hair was disheveled. He looked like he had not slept in days.

"He's sick, *viejo*," Mamá said sadly, glancing up at Papá. "He's been working too hard."

"He has," Papá answered wearily. "This life is killing us all." His eyes watered. He bit his lower lip and walked away.

I felt worse when I remembered that I had to clean the Western Union and be at school on time to welcome the incoming freshmen at the school assembly. "I have to get up," I said. Holding on to Mamá's arm, I slowly stood up. I felt dizzy and weak. I took a few steps but had to stop. I could not stand the pain in my joints and muscles. Mamá helped me back to bed.

"What about the Western Union?" I asked.

"Trampita and I will take care of it," she said, tucking me in. She brought me a glass of water and two aspirins. "You need to rest," she said.

I slept off and on that day and night, and the following afternoon, Mamá drove me to Santa Maria County Hospital.

"I believe you have mononucleosis," the doctor said after examining me.

"Mono *qué?*" Mamá asked, frowning and looking at me. I shrugged my shoulders. I did not understand what he meant either.

"It's a viral infection commonly known as the 'kissing disease,'" he added.

Mamá gave me a funny look. The doctor noticed her and chuckled. "It's called that because the disease can be transmitted by kissing," he said. "It doesn't necessarily mean your son acquired it by kissing." I smiled gratefully at the doctor.

"There's no treatment for mono," the doctor continued. "Get plenty of rest, eat well, drink a lot of water, and take aspirin for your body aches. You should also eat more. You're underweight."

I had a hard time staying in bed and resting. I kept thinking about school and work. I hated missing classes and falling behind. I was afraid to lose my job even though Trampita, Roberto, and Mamá had covered for me. Still feeling worn-out and achy, I dragged myself out of bed Friday morning. I took a long time to get ready. Pain shot up my legs when I moved quickly. I finished cleaning the Western Union after it had opened and was late for school. In study hall, I received a note to go see Mr. Ivan

Muse, the assistant principal in charge of student activities. I figured it had something to do with my duties as student body president. I entered his office, feeling anxious. "Frankie, what happened to you?" he said in his Texas drawl. His dark brownish green sport coat matched the color of his eyes. His receding hairline made him look older than he was. Before I had a chance to answer, he added, "Why weren't you at the freshmen assembly?"

"I've been sick," I answered.

"I can see that," he responded, looking me up and down. "But why didn't you call to let us know?" he added, raising his voice.

"I didn't know who to call. Besides, we don't have a phone." I felt embarrassed. "I am sorry."

Mr. Muse looked me in the eyes and after a long pause said, "I see." He softened his tone of voice and continued, "Well, we waited and waited for you to welcome the freshmen and when you didn't show up, we asked Ernie DeGasparis to do it. He did a fine job."

"I am glad," I said. "I am sure I couldn't have done as good."

"As *well*," he said, correcting me. He must have noticed my face turning red because he quickly added, "Of course you could have done as well."

"Thank you," I said, feeling less uncomfortable.

"Let's get together next month to discuss the agenda for our first meeting with the delegate assembly," he said.

He stood up behind his desk and shook my hand. I was glad our meeting was over.

At the end of the day, I grew more and more tired and listless. I was behind in every course. In my P.E. class I suited up but sat on the bench because I did not have the energy or strength to work out. To make things worse, I did not see Paul Takagi all day. After school I went straight to the public library to study, but I could not concentrate. I kept worrying about all the homework I had to do and the little time I had to do it. At four-thirty I drove home to pick up Trampita. He was excited to help me clean the gas company and not have to work in the fields. Every few minutes I sat down to rest. As I watched him work I thought about how I took care of him in our *Carcachita* when he was a baby while Papá, Mamá, and Roberto picked cotton.

As days went by, I could not keep up with my classes. My midterm grades went down and so did my spirit. I dropped my physics class. I became frustrated and angry. "Perhaps Papá was right when he said he was cursed," I told Mamá one day when I felt like giving up. "Maybe I am cursed too."

"No, *mijo*," she said firmly. "You mustn't believe that, not for a second. Things will get better for you; you must have faith." When she saw I was not responding, she continued. "Remember Torito?"

"What about him?" I asked impatiently.

"Remember when he was sick? The doctors thought he was going to die, but I never believed it. We prayed to the *Santo Niño de Atocha* for a whole year and..."

"And he got well," I said.

"Right," Mamá said, putting her arm around me. "Now you know what you must do."

I began praying on a regular basis once again. Slowly I began to recover and after four weeks I felt much better. Trampita continued helping me at the gas company and Mike Nevel gave him two places to clean on his own, a coffee shop and a pet store. This brought our family extra income, which we badly needed.

Even though Paul Takagi and I could not study together in the public library after school anymore because he had a job in his church, I managed to bring up my grades and carry out my duties as student body president, which were not many. I met with student representatives to the delegate assembly and tried getting everyone involved in promoting school spirit. It was frustrating at times because students did not want to participate in student government.

A Fumble

The only regret I had about being student body president was having lunch with the Rotary Club at the Santa Maria Inn.

After one of our delegate assembly meetings, Mr. Muse informed me that I had been invited to have lunch at the Rotary Club meeting on the following Tuesday. I had no idea what the Rotary Club was, but I figured it was important because Mr. Muse told me to wear a coat and tie. That evening when I got home from work I told Papá and Mamá that I needed to buy one.

"That luncheon is an expensive event," Papá said, frowning. Mamá's eyes shifted back and forth, looking for a response.

"What did you say the name of the club was?" Papá asked.

"Rotary," I responded.

"*Roto*," he said, amused. "How can it be important if it's *roto?*"

"It's Rotary," I repeated, chuckling, "not *torn.*"

"We can buy a jacket at J.C. Penney. It's not too expensive," Mamá said. "Panchito should have a nice coat. He'll get a lot of use out of it."

"I will!" I exclaimed, supporting Mamá's efforts to convince Papá.

"He'll have it for a long time. I don't think he'll grow any more," she said, glancing at me and grinning. I pouted, pretending I was upset. We both laughed and looked at Papá.

"Well, if you want to buy it, go ahead," he said. "But it'll have to be on credit."

I went with Mamá to J.C. Penney and tried on different coats. I liked a dark blue one, but when we checked the price tag, Mamá and I convinced ourselves it did not fit right. We finally settled on a dark green and brown checked coat that was on sale. We looked for ties to match and found a perfect one, but I could not tie it because I did not know how. I ended up getting a clip-on. We also bought a white shirt. Tuesday morning when I wore my new outfit, Papá told me I looked important.

At the end of the last class before lunch, I headed for Mr. Muse's office. I was to meet him there to go with him to the Rotary Club luncheon at the Santa Maria Inn, which was right across the street from the high school.

"You look very nice," Mr. Muse said as I walked into his office.

"Thanks," I responded, focusing on his beautiful dark blue suit. I noticed his tie was not a clip-on and wondered how he tied it.

"What's the Rotary Club?" I asked, remembering Papá's comment and chuckling to myself.

"It's an international club for business and professional people, like the mayor of Santa Maria and the president of Bank of America," he responded. The thought of having lunch with so many important people made me nervous. As we approached the inn, I noticed colorful flowers, shrubs, and ferns all around the building. Mr. Muse buttoned his coat as we entered. I buttoned mine too. The lobby was full of men dressed in suits or sport coats standing in small groups, drinking, talking, and laughing. The noise got louder as more men came in. Mr. Muse excused himself to say hello to a friend. I put my hands in my pant pockets and walked around, admiring the stained-glass windows and the paintings on the warm wooden walls. I then went out to the patio. It was filled with sun and shade. The gentle sounds of water cascading from the fountain reminded me of the creek that ran behind our cabin in the cotton labor camp in Corcoran. I went back in the lobby and looked for Mr. Muse. I spotted him standing by himself. I walked up and stood by his side. "We'll be called pretty soon," he said, glancing around the room. Then a short, pudgy man ringing a cowbell bolted out from the middle of a crowd.

"Time to eat!" he shouted. "If you're not in the dining room by the time I count to ten, you'll have to pay a fine." Laughter and hoots filled the air. The men moved quickly to the dining room. Mr. Muse and I lined up behind them. "One . . . ten!" the man with the cowbell yelled in Mr. Muse's face.

"It's not fair. You didn't count to ten," Mr. Muse said, laughing and turning red like a tomato.

"You owe me two bucks," the man hollered. "One for being late and another for talking back!" Mr. Muse took out his wallet and gave him two dollars. The man went around the dining room making up reasons for fining people. Everyone thought it was hilarious, but I did not understand it. I thought important men were supposed to be more polite and mannerly.

Mr. Muse and I sat at a table with two other men who talked about business. Mr. Muse mostly listened and peppered their conversation with brief comments. Once in a while they glanced at me and smiled. I nervously smiled back. I looked at the table setting and was confused when I saw two forks, one smaller than the other. I waited for Mr. Muse to start. He picked up the small fork. I did the same. I followed every move he made, hoping he would not notice. When the dessert came, I sighed. I knew the lunch was soon to be over. I looked out the dining room window into the courtyard and watched a man pulling out weeds on his knees. His face was dark and weather-beaten. He reminded me of Papá. I felt a knot in my throat. The ringing of the cowbell pulled my attention back inside. Everyone's eyes focused on a man behind the podium who identified himself as the president of the Rotary Club. After making endless announcements, he welcomed visiting Rotary Club members from other cities and began introducing invited guests, who stood up as their names were called. As soon as I heard my name I jumped up, and, before he finished introducing me, I sat down again.

"He's the student body president at Santa Maria High School. Come up and say a few words, Frankie," he said, motioning with his hand for me to approach the podium. "Tell us something about your school." I was shocked, terrified. I did not know I had to speak. I sat petrified, wishing that I had heard wrong.

"Go on," Mr. Muse said, giving me a gentle shove. I slowly walked up, went behind the podium, and grabbed on to it. I felt dizzy and had a sudden pain in the side of my stomach. I could hear my heart pounding as I glanced up at the audience. My mind went blank. I could hear my own silence. My face felt on fire and my legs trembled uncontrollably. Words slowly began to come out of my mouth, but I had no control over them. Spanish words wove with English words like braids. I knew I was not making any sense when I saw Mr. Muse frowning and staring at me as though he were seeing an animal with two heads. I finally managed to stop myself from babbling. I caught my breath, said a few words about student government, and rushed back to my seat, wishing I could disappear.

"I am sorry, Mr. Muse," I said as we walked back to school. "I was so nervous, but..."

"Yes, you were," he said, interrupting me.

"But I didn't know I had to speak," I responded, trying to justify my poor performance.

"I didn't either," he said apologetically. "Don't worry about it. Forget it."

I tried to forget it, but I could not. Every time I relived that experience, I got angry with the president of the Rotary Club. *He should have asked me ahead of time*, I thought. I dreamed about that lunch often and when I did I was glad to wake up. In one of my dreams I gave the talk entirely in Spanish. It was clear and smooth. That time I was sorry to wake up.

A Breakthrough

At the beginning of the second semester of my senior year, many of my classmates were excited about going to college. They talked about it in the library, the cafeteria, and study hall. Some were going to the University of California at Santa Barbara or UCLA. Others got into Fresno State but were waiting to hear from Berkeley. I did not share their enthusiasm. I had to stay home and continue helping my family. Whenever they asked me what college I was planning to attend, I told them Cal Poly San Luis Obispo. I did not tell them when because I did not know.

On Wednesday, February 17, I was called in to see Mr. Robert Penney, one of the counselors for the senior class. As soon as I walked into his small, clean office, he stood up behind his desk and introduced himself. He was a tall, thin man with sparse black hair, a wide forehead, large blue eyes, and perfect white teeth.

"Let's take a walk to the cafeteria," he said, picking up a folder. I followed him, trying to keep up with his quick, long strides. "Would you like some coffee?" he asked as he poured himself a cup.

"No, thank you, I don't drink coffee."

"Good for you," he responded. He took several sips, refilled it, turned around, and headed out to the parking lot. "Follow me," he said. *This is strange*, I thought. He went up to a white Volkswagen van, unlocked it, and asked me to get in. He started the motor and picked up a tobacco pipe from the dashboard, packed in fresh tobacco, and lit it. "I've got a few errands to make," he said, handing me the folder. "We can talk on the way. I hope it's okay with you. He shifted to high gear and drove down Broadway.

"Sure," I said. I had no idea what he had in mind.

"What colleges have you applied to?" he asked as he parked in front of the Bank of America.

"None."

"You're joking." He took a puff and placed the thick black pipe on the ashtray.

"I am not," I said sadly, looking out the window. "I can't afford it."

"Sure you can," he assured me. I have a few scholarship applications for you to fill out. They're in this folder.

Take a look at them. I am going to the bank. I'll be right back."

I opened the folder and leafed through the pile of applications: the Madrinas Club Scholarship, Bank of America Scholarship, Lions Club Scholarship, Santa Maria Valley Scholarship. I gulped when I saw the one for the Rotary Club. I pulled it out and placed it at the bottom of the pile. I continued looking through them until Mr. Penney returned.

"I consulted with your previous counselor, Mr. Kinkade," he said, sliding into the driver's seat. "We agreed you have an excellent chance of getting some of those scholarships. Now, let's talk about colleges." At this point I wanted to explain my situation at home, but Mr. Penney kept on talking. I did not interrupt him because I knew it was bad manners. "The application deadlines for some have passed, but I'll check when we get back to my office. You'll also need to take the SAT. I've signed you up for it." He paused for a second, chuckled, and added, "You have a lot of work to do!" At this point I felt tired and discouraged. He looked at me from the corner of his eye and said, "What's the matter? You don't seem happy."

"I appreciate your help," I said. "But even if I get all these scholarships, I won't be able to go to college. My family needs me."

"I know your family will miss you," he said sympathetically.

"No, I mean, I have to support them," I said. Mr. Penney looked surprised and confused. I felt uncomfortable telling him about my home situation because Papá had taught us to keep our family life private, but I thought he needed to know. After all, he was going out of his way to help me. I finished my story back at his office.

"I had no idea . . . it's quite unusual," he said, scratching his forehead with the stem of his pipe. "But I am sure we can figure something out." He canceled his next appointment and wrote me an absence excuse for my next class, which was California history. He paced his office, holding his pipe in the palm of his left hand and rubbing it with his thumb. "What about your younger brother, the one you said sometimes helps you at work, what's his name?" he asked, looking out the window.

"José Francisco, but we call him 'Trampita.'"

"Could Trompita take over your job?" he asked, mispronouncing my brother's nickname.

"I hadn't thought of that!" I exclaimed. "I think Trampita can do it. He's been helping me a lot already and Mike Nevel likes him."

"Who's Mike Nevel?"

"My boss, the owner of Santa Maria Window Cleaners. I need to ask him." I then remembered I also had to ask Papá. My excitement slowly faded. Who knew what Papá would say? "I have to discuss the idea with my family and get my father's permission," I said. "It's not going to be easy."

"I'd be happy to talk with your father," he responded.

"He doesn't speak English," I said. "Do you speak Spanish?"

"No, I don't. Look, talk to your family about this. Meantime, take those applications, fill them out, and bring them back to me during your study hall class next Monday."

That afternoon I went to work excited and hopeful. I finished cleaning the gas company and went home, happy but anxious. *I hope Papá is in a good mood,* I thought. As I walked in the door, Mamá greeted me and heated dinner for me. "I need to talk to you and Papá," I said, pushing my plate away. "Is Trampita awake? I have to talk to him too."

"Is something wrong, *mijo?*" Mamá asked.

"No, I have to get your permission on something," I said.

"You're getting married," Mamá said jokingly. We both laughed. Papá came out of his room.

"What's all the noise about?" he grumbled.

"Panchito has something to ask us," she said cheerfully. "I'll go get Trampita. He and Torito just went to bed."

Papá sat at the kitchen table, lit a cigarette, and asked me to bring him a glass of water and two aspirins. I knew his mood was not in my favor. Mamá returned with Trampita. My brother sat at the table next to me, facing Papá and Mamá.

Papá puffed on his cigarette and stared at his right hand with the missing finger. "Okay, what is it?" he snapped, breaking the silence.

I hooked my feet around the legs of the chair, locked my hands together underneath the table, and began telling them the plan Mr. Penney and I discussed. I avoided Papá's eyes while I talked and focused on Mamá's smile. When I finished, Papá grumbled, "Let's think about it." He bit his lower lip and shifted his body to the side, away from me.

"I can do it," Trampita said proudly.

"It's a wonderful opportunity," Mamá said.

"Didn't you hear me?" Papá shouted. "I said let's think about it!"

Blood rushed to my head. My knuckles turned white and ached, just like my jaw. Anger swallowed me and I could not escape it. "Think about what!" I cried out. "It's my only chance!"

"Your chance?" Papá fired back. His eyes pierced right through me. His lower lip bled as he bit into it. "It's your chance to shut up. *Eres un malcriado!* Don't they teach you respect at school, ah?"

Trampita excused himself and ran back to his room. Mamá signaled for me to stop, but I could not.

"It's my only chance!" I repeated, trying to hold back my tears.

Papá winced as he stood up. His face was as white as a ghost's. "Shut your mouth, Pancho, or I'll shut it for you," he said, shaking.

"Please, *viejo*," Mamá said, moving closer to him.

"You stay out of it!" he yelled, pushing her away. He lifted his hand, threatening to strike her.

"Don't! Leave her alone!" I shouted instinctively. My anger turned into fear. Papá turned around and slapped me on the side of the face with the back of his right hand. I was stunned. My face felt like it was on fire.

"Stop, for God's sake!" Mamá cried out at Papá.

Papá gave me a pained look, hobbled to his room, and shut the door. I rested my head on the table and wept. Mamá sat next to me and put her arm around my shoulders.

"Are you okay, Panchito?"

I nodded. "Why can't he understand?" I said, wiping my tears and my runny nose on my shirtsleeves.

"He does, *mijo*, but he doesn't want to lose you too." Tears rolled down her face. "Your Papá wants the family to be together. He doesn't want his children to leave. First, Roberto left when he got married. Now, if you go to college, you'll leave too. It hurts him. It hurts him too that he can't support the family. His dream to earn and save enough money and eventually to return to Mexico with all of us is gone."

"I think I understand, Mamá. But what about my dream?"

"I know what you mean, *mijo*," she said, stroking the back of my head. "Have faith in God. I'll talk to your father tomorrow when he feels better. Remember, he didn't say no. That's a good sign. Now go outside to get some fresh air and go to bed. You need to rest."

I went outside and looked up at the stars. I felt a pain in my chest. That night I did not sleep and neither did Mamá. I heard her murmuring prayers for a long time.

On Friday morning I had a hard time getting out of bed. I felt tired and depressed. I skipped breakfast and went to work in a daze. The clicking noise of telegraph machines at the Western Union seemed distant. I went from class to class, not paying attention to anything that was said or discussed. After school, I went to the public library but could not focus on my homework. I thought about the night before and wished it had never happened. I took a walk around the library gardens, trying to figure out what to do. I thought about Papá and felt guilty. Perhaps I was being selfish. Perhaps I was not being fair to my family, especially Trampita. I walked back to the library, picked up my books, and headed for the gas company. While I dusted and swept the floors, I kept thinking of how tired and bored I was working for Santa Maria

Window Cleaners day in and day out. I did not want to do this for the rest of my life.

I went home late that evening, expecting everyone to be asleep. To my surprise, Mamá was sitting on the front steps waiting for me. As soon as I climbed out of the car, she ran up to me and gave me a hug. "*Mijo*, I have good news!" she said excitedly. "Your father has agreed!"

"Really?" I exclaimed. "Where's Papá?"

"In his room, asleep. He had a very hard day."

"You did it, Mamá! You did it! Thank you!" I said, jumping up and down.

"*Gracias a Dios y al maestro* Osterveen," she said.

"Mr. Osterveen, the Spanish teacher?" I asked, puzzled.

"He came this afternoon and talked to your Papá and me. He said your counselor..." Mamá hesitated, trying to remember his name.

"Mr. Penney," I said.

"Yes, Mr. Penney. What a strange name...Why would they name him *Centavo?* Anyway, he asked Mr. Osterveen to talk to us... *Es buena gente.* We couldn't believe that an important person like him would visit us. He and Papá talked about Mexico. His wife is from Oaxaca, you know, and he lived there for many years. He went on and on talking about college and you. *Habló como perico.* Papá and I didn't understand a lot of what he said about college, but we felt really proud about all the nice things he said about you."

We quietly went into the house. "I think I heard your Papá cough. He might be awake now," Mamá said. I slowly opened the door to his room and peeked in. He was lying on his back, still asleep, with both arms on top of the covers and crossed over his chest. I tiptoed in, kneeled on his bedside, and watched him. He looked haggard. I gently kissed his hands and thanked him under my breath.

That weekend, I filled out the scholarship applications and took them to Mr. Penney on Monday morning during my study hall period. After I thanked him for what he did to convince my father, he gave me some bad news: it was too late to apply to most colleges for the fall. "I suggest you apply to the University of Santa Clara," he said.

I had never heard of the University of Santa Clara. Mr. Penney must have noticed my lack of enthusiasm because he quickly added, "You'll like it. It's a lot like Loyola, my alma mater."

"Your alma mater?" I asked, not knowing what he meant.

"The school I went to in L.A.," he responded. "Santa Clara is small like Loyola. It has a good academic reputation."

"Smaller than Cal Poly?" I asked.

"Much smaller. You won't get lost there. It's a small Jesuit Catholic school."

The fact that it was Catholic attracted me. I knew Mamá would like it too. "Where is it?" I asked.

"Up north, near San Jose. It's only about 250 miles, so you'll get a chance to come home on holidays," he said. I was definitely interested. I did not want to be too far from my family in case they needed me.

"Can I get a job there?" I asked, thinking I could help my family.

"I know where you're heading with this," he said, smiling. "Sure, but you'll need to concentrate on your studies. You won't have time to work and get involved in extra-curricular activities like you have here." Mr. Penney picked up his pipe, filled it with tobacco from a small pouch, and lit it. The smell of sweet cherry filled the air. "Are you interested in applying?" he asked, handing me the application.

"Yes!" I said enthusiastically.

"Good! I figured you would be." His eyes twinkled.

I glanced at the application. My heart sank to my stomach when I saw the deadline had past.

"Don't worry about the deadline," he said, noticing the shock on my face. "I called Santa Clara this morning and asked my friend at admissions to give you an extension." I sighed in relief. Mr. Penney chuckled and puffed on his pipe. I floated out of his office thinking my counselor was like the *Santo Niño de Atocha*, the Holy Child of a thousand wonders.

I took the SAT test at Cal Poly on Saturday morning, March eighth. I had a hard time sleeping the night before because I was worried about the test. When I finally dozed off, I dreamed I was waxing the floors at the gas company. I kept glancing at the clock on the wall because I did not want to be late for the test. When it was time to leave, I could not move. My feet were glued to the floor. I dropped the mop and tried to reach out to grab a desk, but I could not lift my arms. They felt like lead. I looked out the window and saw Papá and Roberto picking strawberries. I cried out to them for help, but they could not hear me. I woke up in a sweat. My heart was racing. I could not go back to sleep, so I got up and headed for the Western Union. After I finished cleaning it, I rushed to Cal Poly to take the exam.

The test consisted of three parts: two on English and one on math. I would have preferred one on English and two on math, but luck was not on my side. When I found out my combined scores were slightly below nine hundred, with math being higher than English, I was disappointed, but I was relieved when Mr. Penney told me I had done better than he had expected.

Graduation Day

The day I received the letter from the University of Santa Clara notifying me that I had been accepted, I was as excited as the day my parents returned from Mexico after we had been deported. I read the letter over and over to myself and to my family.

My excitement, however, turned to concern when I saw the cost for the first year was two thousand dollars. I did not tell my parents because I did not want them to worry too. I took the letter to Mr. Penney and thanked him for helping me get into college.

"Don't thank me; you did it on your own," he said.

"Yes, but..."

"No buts," he said, interrupting me. "You worked hard. You don't owe me anything."

I disagreed with him, but I did not insist. I knew Mr.

Penney felt uncomfortable whenever I thanked him. I then mentioned the high cost.

"No reason to be concerned. You'll get scholarships," he said confidently.

"Two thousand dollars?" I said worriedly.

Mr. Penney took a puff on his pipe and placed it on the ashtray. He stared out the window and said: "Unfortunately, you applied too late to the University of Santa Clara to qualify for financial aid but, hopefully, the scholarships you receive from local organizations will cover your first year."

"What if they don't?" I said, feeling anxious.

"You can borrow the rest from the federal government," he said, handing me a National Defense Student Loan application. "Their loans carry very low interest rates, and if you go into teaching they'll forgive ten percent of the loan for every year you teach, up to fifty percent."

"I do want to be a teacher," I said, "but my parents won't like the idea of borrowing money."

"The loan will be yours, not theirs, and you won't have to begin paying it until you have a job teaching."

It sounded good, but I still felt uneasy. Papá said that borrowing money was like being enslaved. He told us about an *hacendado*, a large landowner, who used his company store to keep his father and other peasants in a state of endless debt. However, I trusted Mr. Penney and agreed to apply for the loan.

"How much should I apply for?" I asked.

Mr. Penney picked up his pipe, tapped it lightly against the ashtray, and rolled his eyes to the back of his head, looking for the right figure. "Why don't you apply for one thousand?" he said, bringing his pipe to a standstill and glancing at me.

I gulped and glanced at Mr. Penney, who was waiting for my response. I lowered my eyes and noticed a stain on the carpet. *I would have to clean floors for a thousand hours to earn a thousand dollars,* I thought. I looked up at Mr. Penney and said, "It's a lot of money, but worth it."

"That's the spirit."

I took the application home and began filling it out at the kitchen table. When I got to the line that asked for the place of birth, I suddenly felt the same suffocating fear I had felt for many years of being caught by *la migra.* I heard Papá's voice in my head: "You can't tell a soul you were born in Mexico. You can't trust anyone, not even your best friends. If they know, they'll turn you in." *But I am here legally,* I thought. *I have my green card.* I left that line blank and continued filling out the application. When I finished, I checked it over for mistakes, folded it, placed it in the envelope, and went to bed. I had a hard time falling asleep. I kept hearing Papá's voice and reliving the frightening immigration raids in Tent City and Corcoran. The next morning, at work, I completed the application. Next to place of birth, I wrote in Colton, California.

After I had turned in the scholarship and NDSL loan applications, I rushed home after work and anxiously checked the mail every day. As soon as I walked in the door, I would ask Mamá, "Did I get any mail?" "No, *mijo*, not today," she would say. As days went by, she would meet me at the door and before I had a chance to ask, she would imitate me, saying, "Did I get any mail?" She would smile when the answer was no and then try to cheer me up. "You need to be more patient, Panchito," she would say. "It'll come; I've been praying." Her words helped, but I could not stop worrying. I remembered Mr. Penney saying, "With your school record, you won't have any problem getting scholarships." I calculated my grade point average, 3.77, and prayed and hoped that my counselor was right.

On June 1, 1962, I got the news. I arrived home from work that evening and found Mamá waiting for me on the front steps, waving a white envelope. I was so anxious to get the mail that I accidentally tripped over one of the stray dogs that followed me as I got out of the car. "You got mail, *mijo*," Mamá said, smiling from ear to ear. I snatched the envelope from her and ripped it open. The letter was from Mr. Paul Rosendahl, director of guidance and chairman of scholarships at Santa Maria High School. "What's it say?" Mamá asked excitedly. I quickly scanned the letter and started jumping up and down.

"I got the Alegría Scholarship for three hundred and fifty dollars; the Kiwanis Club for two hundred and fifty; the Lions Club for two hundred; and the Madrinas Club for two hundred!" I exclaimed.

"*Gracias a Dios!*" Mamá said, folding her hands and looking up at the heavens. She gave me a big hug and lightly pushed me inside the house. Our excitement had woken up Papá. He came out of his room and slowly sat down at the kitchen table.

"*Qué escándalo es éste?*" he asked. Trampita, Torito, Rorra, and Rubén all came out running to see what was going on.

"Panchito got money for school!" Mamá shouted, a bit out of breath. "Tell them, *mijo*, tell them."

"I got one thousand dollars for school," I said excitedly.

"It pays to work hard, *mijo*," Papá said, lighting up a Camel cigarette.

"Let me see the money," Rorra said, pulling on my left arm.

"They'll send it to me when I am in college," I told her, chuckling.

"Yes, when he *goes away* to college," Papá uttered wearily. His eyes watered.

"Okay, everyone back to bed. It's late," Mamá said. "Papá needs to rest, so be quiet." She followed behind my brothers and sister, making sure they went back to bed. Papá winced as he got up from the chair and shuffled back to his room. He had a sad look on his face.

The following day, I got another bit of good news in the mail. Frank Schneider, director of financial aid at the University of Santa Clara, notified me that my National Defense Student Loan application for one thousand dollars had been approved. I now had enough money for my first year of college.

The school year was coming to an end and, for the first time, I did not feel sad about it. I looked forward to graduation.

The ceremony was on Thursday evening, June seventh, at eight o'clock at Wilson Gym. At five o'clock that day, Roberto, Trampita, Torito, and I worked as a team and began cleaning the gas company as soon as it closed. At six-thirty I rushed home to get ready and pick up my parents. My brothers stayed behind to finish. They were to leave after work, pick up Darlene, Rorra, and Rubén, and go directly to the gym. I was excited and nervous. I was to lead the flag salute and give the welcome at the graduation ceremonies. I felt proud and hoped my parents could attend, but I was not sure they would.

I remembered that neither of them had gone to Roberto's high school graduation. That day Papá complained about a terrible headache and his back, and insisted Mamá stay home to take care of him and the children. My brother felt hurt, but he said he understood.

For graduation, Papá gave him an old ring that belonged to my grandfather. Roberto wore his ring proudly. I think his ring meant as much to him as my Saint Christopher medal meant to me.

I did not want to give my parents the choice of saying no, so as soon as I entered the house, I said, "Are you ready? We have to be there by seven-thirty." Papá and Mamá were sitting at the kitchen table talking. Before they had a chance to say anything, I quickly went into the shed, took a quick, cold bath in the aluminum tub, and got dressed. When I came out, Mamá was getting ready, but not Papá. "Get me a couple of aspirins, *mijo*. My head is killing me," he said, covering his head with both hands.

I brought him three aspirins and a glass of water. "Here you are," I said. "Your headache will be gone in no time. By the time we get there you'll feel fine."

"I don't think I can go, Panchito," he said, rubbing the back of his neck. "I am not feeling well. Besides, I don't speak English; I don't know anyone and..."

"You won't be the only one who doesn't speak or understand English," I said. Papá was noticeably upset that I had interrupted him. He gave me an angry look. I softened my voice and pleaded, "Please, Papá, it means a lot to me." Papá lowered his head and thought for a moment.

"What would I wear?" he asked.

"You can wear my white shirt and tie," I said happily, thinking that he was giving in.

Mamá must have heard us, because she brought out the white shirt and tie I wore at the Rotary Club luncheon. Papá grinned and slowly got up from the table. "Here, *viejo*, let me help you," she said, unbuttoning Papá's shirt and helping him to take it off. While Mamá helped him put on the white shirt, I slipped into my graduation gown and put on my white silk California Scholarship Federation sash. "You look like a priest," Papá said, chuckling.

"He'd make a good one," Mamá said.

The shirt was a bit too big for Papá. It made him look thinner and the whiteness made the dark circles under his eyes stand out even more. I then helped him put on the tie. "*Esto parece babero,*" Papá said.

"It's a tie, not a bib," Mamá said, laughing.

"It makes me look important," he said.

"You are important, *viejo*," Mamá responded. Papá looked up at her and grinned.

It was the first time I had ever seen him wear a shirt and tie. He looked strange to me, but handsome. I looked at the clock. It was getting late and Papá had not changed his pants and shoes.

"You go ahead, *mijo*," Papá said, noticing my nervousness. "Don't wait for us; *vieja* and I will get a ride with Joe and Espy."

"No, I'll wait for you; it'll only take a few more minutes."

"You can't be late," he said firmly. "You should leave now."

I did not want to leave without them. I was afraid that Papá would change his mind after I left and end up not going. "I'll wait," I responded.

"Go, I said!" Papá shot back. I had annoyed him with my insistence. Mamá caught my eye and signaled for me not to argue.

"Go ahead, *mijo*, do as your father says," she said. "We'll meet you there."

I picked up my cap and left, not knowing whether or not Papá would attend. I got to the gym a few minutes before the procession. I moved up to the front of the line to join my classmates who had also made the California Scholarship Federation every semester for four years. We marched up the middle of the aisle, banked on both sides by rows of seats reserved for our graduating class. I sat in the front row, facing a low platform that served as the stage. After the Reverend Glen Johnson from the Gloria Dei Lutheran Church gave the invocation and benediction, I was introduced. I walked up to the podium, feeling nervous but confident. I quickly scanned the bleachers, hoping to see my family, and began: "I pledge allegiance to the flag of the United States of America and to the Republic for which it stands, one nation under God... with liberty and justice for all." I could hardly hear my

own voice as thousands of others joined and recited it
with me. It sounded like a prayer in church. As I finished,
I saw Papá and Mamá entering through the door in the
back of the gym. My father braced himself on my mother's
shoulder. My heart raced with excitement. I smiled, took
a deep breath, and proudly gave the welcome.

Still Moving

Little changed for my family and me during the summer after graduation. I worked for Santa Maria Window Cleaners, helping Mike Nevel during the day and doing my regular job in the evenings and on weekends. Trampita worked for Mike Nevel and often helped me in the evenings. Torito picked strawberries for Ito, and Mamá ironed for migrant families and took care of their babies. She also looked after Rorra, Rubén, and Papá.

What did change was the size of my brother's family. Roberto and Darlene had a beautiful baby girl who brought joy and new life to our whole family. My parents doted on her. Papá bragged about how much little Jackie resembled the Jiménezes. Mamá naturally agreed with Papá, but she insisted that Jackie also looked like my brother's wife. Trampita, Torito, and I argued about who Jackie's favorite uncle was. We never agreed, even after

I had convinced Rorra and Rubén to take my side.

All summer, I marked off the days on a calendar that hung on our kitchen wall. The calendar had a picture of a colorful Aztec warrior standing guard over an Aztec princess whose eyes were closed; both were dressed in plumed and colorful costumes. One morning I asked Papá and Mamá if they knew the story behind the picture.

"Vaguely," Papá said. "I think the warrior thought the princess was asleep, but she was dead."

"No, she wasn't dead," Mamá said. "She was asleep and the warrior protected her while she dreamed." I liked Mamá's answer better and I wondered what the princess dreamed about. For each day I crossed out, my excitement and anxiety grew stronger.

The day I had been waiting for finally arrived. It was Sunday of the first week of September. I woke up at dawn feeling excited about making the trip to Santa Clara. This was the first time in my life I did not feel sad about moving. I quietly got up and went in the shed to bathe in the aluminum tub. Soon I would be taking hot showers in college, just like I did in my P.E. classes in high school. By the time I had finished getting dressed, Mamá was already preparing breakfast and the lunch for our trip. I went back to my room and began sorting and folding my clothes, trying not to disturb Torito and Rubén, who were still asleep. They slept together in the twin bed next to mine, which I had shared with Roberto when he lived with us. Mamá walked in with Rorra and woke up my brothers. "Time to get up, *flojos*," she said, pulling the blankets off of them. "Look, Rorra is already up." My sister stood next to Mamá looking smug. The boys moaned, rubbed their eyes, and pulled up the covers. "Come on, *mijos*. You've got to get going if you want to come with us to take Panchito to Santa Clara." Torito and Rubén jumped out of bed.

"Rubén looks like a chihuahua dog in underwear," Torito said, laughing and pointing at my youngest brother. Rubén made a face and stuck his tongue out at Torito.

"*Ándale, malcriado*," Mamá said, chuckling and pinching Torito's behind. He leaped like a rabbit and ran to the kitchen. Rubén and Rorra ran behind him. Mamá picked up one of my shirts and began folding it. She was quiet and pensive until she heard Papá.

"*Vieja! Vieja!*" he shouted from his room.

"Yes, *viejo*, I am coming!" Mamá hollered, placing my shirt in the box. She smoothed it with her right hand and sighed. "Papá needs help getting dressed," she said. "I'll be right back." Rorra followed her like a shadow. A few minutes later, Mamá returned carrying a bundle of new clothes. Her eyes sparkled and she was smiling from ear to ear.

"What's this?" I exclaimed.

"I bought you some new clothes," she said excitedly. "I wanted to surprise you, *mijo*."

"Thank you!" I said. My eyes watered. Mamá tried to hold back her tears as she handed me the clothes: two pairs of pants, one navy blue, one black; a couple of short-sleeved shirts; three pairs of white underwear; and a pair of low, black, pointed boots.

"You like them?" Mamá asked hopefully.

"Of course," I said, "but..."

"How did I pay for them?" she said, anticipating my question. "Ay, Panchito, *como eres Preguntón.* You've always been nosy; always asking questions, even when you were a little boy," she said, chuckling. "You're worse than your father." She paused, thought about it for a moment, and added, "Okay, I'll tell you. I've been saving a little bit every week from groceries. But don't worry, *mijo,* they didn't cost much. J.C. Penney had a good back-to-school sale."

"Thank you, Mamá," I said, giving her a hug.

At that point, Trampita came into the room. He had just returned from cleaning the Western Union and Pat's Pets.

"Thanks, Trampita," I said. "I wouldn't be able to go to college if you didn't take over my job."

"Don't feel bad," he said, trying to cheer me up. "I get to keep your car. Now, if you gave me those *nice* boots, we'd be even," he added.

"What's wrong with my boots?" I said.

"With those sharp toes you can kill cockroaches in corners!" he said, snickering.

I picked up one of the boots and threatened to throw it at him. He flew out of the room, laughing. Mamá went back to the kitchen to check on my brothers and sister. I continued folding my clothes and putting them in the box. After I finished packing, I wrote a note to Trampita to thank and surprise him. I placed it underneath his pillow, along with my copper pyrite rock for good luck. I then carried the box out to the car and loaded it in the trunk. The cool fog caressed my face. I took a deep breath and went back inside the house.

Mamá grabbed me by the arm and took me aside. "Papá is in a really bad mood," she whispered. "He hates to see you go. But don't let it get to you. Be patient with him like you've always been."

"Don't worry, Mamá, I understand."

Papá sat at the kitchen table, smoking a cigarette and staring out into space. Once again, he looked haggard. His eyes were puffy and red. I greeted him and sat across from him to eat breakfast. He glanced at me and feigned a smile. Mamá stood at the kitchen sink washing dishes. She kept shifting her weight from one leg to the other, trying to ease the pain from the swelling of her varicose veins.

"*Ándele, viejo, coma algo,*" she said tenderly, trying to get Papá to eat something. He finally drank a glass of milk and ate cottage cheese with bananas. He liked to eat dairy products because he said they helped ease his stomach pains.

Everyone was ready to leave. We secured the front door with a padlock and stood outside by the car, waiting for Roberto, Darlene, and Jackie to arrive to say good-bye. As soon as I saw them, I felt a lump in my throat. My brother parked his car behind ours. His eyes turned red and watery as we approached and hugged each other. We were silent. Each one of us knew what the other was feeling.

"You'll see each other for Christmas," Darlene said, rubbing my brother's broad shoulders with her right hand.

"Where's little Jackie?" I asked, finally letting go of my brother and wiping my tears with the back of my hand.

"She's asleep in the back seat of the car," Roberto answered. His thick lower lip quivered.

Darlene went to the car and brought little Jackie, wrapped in a pink blanket, in her arms. I gave the baby a light kiss, and she opened her eyes and cooed. "That's your favorite uncle," Darlene said to Jackie. "Say hi." The baby smiled.

"*Vámonos, pues*," Papá said impatiently, motioning to us to get going. Mamá, Trampita, Rubén, and Rorra climbed in. Papá slowly slid into the passenger's seat, wincing and holding on to Roberto's muscular arms. I got in the driver's seat, secured the door, and drove away, waving good-bye. The car bounced up and down as it hit the potholes in the dirt path leading out of Bonetti Ranch. A pack of stray, skinny dogs followed us, barking at the wheels and waking up the few neighbors who did not work on Sundays.

The sun was beginning to come up over the hills as I turned onto East Main Street and headed toward Santa Maria to catch highway 101. A few minutes later, I glanced at the rearview mirror. Mamá had fallen asleep with her right arm around Torito, Rubén, and Rorra. I fixed my eyes ahead on the long, straight road, which cut through hundreds of green fields that stretched for miles on either side. It looked like a black strip on a plush green carpet. At a short distance, to my left, I saw several men and women picking strawberries on their knees and children playing near old, dusty cars parked at the edge of the field. I glanced at Papá, who winced as he napped on Trampita's shoulder. I felt sad and then angry. I clenched the steering wheel and hit the accelerator. The car jerked and woke up Papá.

"Slow down, Pancho!" he said angrily. "What's the matter with you?"

"Nothing, Papá, I am in control." I took my foot from the accelerator and lightly pressed on the brakes.

"In control, nothing," he said, holding on to the dashboard.

"Look, we're almost in Santa Maria," I said, trying to distract him.

"Sure, we'll be in the cemetery in no time, if you keep driving like this," he said.

"What's wrong?" Mamá said, waking up.

"Ask your son," Papá said, annoyed. "He thinks he's in a car race."

"I got distracted," I said apologetically.

"Let me drive," Trampita said. "You must be too tired."

"I'm fine," I responded. "You need to rest; you'll be driving all the way back to Santa Maria."

As we entered the city of Santa Maria and went by a large, two-story brick house, Mamá said, "Look at that house to your left. Every time I go by it, I wonder what it's like to live in it. Actually, I wonder what it's like living in a house, any house. Maybe someday, *si Dios quiere*."

Papá mumbled something under his breath. Mamá quickly added, "Oh, I don't mind where we live now. It's better than the old garages or tents where we used to live. Maybe Panchito will buy us a house when he finishes college and makes a lot of money. *Verdad, mijo?*"

"Right," I responded, wanting to please Mamá. I had no idea how much money teachers made or how much houses cost.

Driving by Main Street Elementary School brought back memories. It was the same school where I failed first grade because I did not know English well enough and where I had received first prize for my drawing of a butterfly. I felt the same sorrow and happiness I felt then, even though many years had gone by. At the corner of East Main and Broadway, we turned right. Along the way I saw store windows that I had cleaned for Santa Maria Window Cleaners. As we approached the Santa Maria Bridge, I remembered the pain I felt in my chest every time we crossed this bridge, at the end of every summer, on our way north to pick grapes and cotton in Fresno. But this time I felt excitement, not pain — the same feeling I had as a child when my family and I took the train north from Guadalajara, crossed *la frontera,* and entered California.

I speeded up, crossed the bridge, and headed north to Santa Clara. I was going to college. After so many years, I was still moving.

A Note from the Author

Breaking Through, the sequel to *The Circuit*, is autobiographical. It spans crucial years of my young adult life, beginning with the deportation of my family and me back to Mexico. Relying heavily on memory, I selected those meaningful events and experiences in my life that built up to an integrated pattern. I recounted them in chronological order from the perspective of the teenager I was then. I made use of my powers of imagination and invention to fill in small details that I have forgotten with the passage of time. For example, when I could not remember exact words of some conversations, I created dialogue, and I added description to capture my impressions and reactions to particular events and experiences.

In addition to relying on the power of memory, I used other valuable resources to write my book. I interviewed family members and looked through family photographs and documents, including deportation papers, which I obtained through the Freedom of Information Act. I also made use of my junior high and high school records and read through *The Breeze*, the Santa Maria High School student newspaper, and the *Santa Maria Times*. I also visited the Santa Maria Historical Museum.

I wrote this sequel to pay tribute to my family and teachers and to document part of my own history, but, more importantly, to voice the experiences of many children and young adults who confront numerous obstacles in their efforts to "break through ... and become butterflies." How they manage to break through depends as much on their courage, hope, and God-given talents as it does on the loving, compassionate, and generous people who commit themselves to making a difference in the lives of children and young adults.

José Francisco
(Trampita) and
Roberto, picking
plums in Orosi,
California

Francisco, José Francisco (Trampita), and Roberto,
Tent City, Santa Maria, California

Papá, Trampita, and neighbor
Don Pancho at Bonetti Ranch,
Santa Maria, California

Roberto and Francisco
with their mother,
Joaquina, in the cotton
fields of Corcoran

Francisco, freshman at Santa Maria High School

Francisco, singing "Cielito Lindo" for Junior Scandals, Santa Maria High School

Paul Takagi, student body treasurer, and Francisco, student body president, Santa Maria High School

Francisco Jiménez immigrated with his family to California from Tlaquepaque, Mexico. He worked in the fields of California as a child, and his autobiographical novel, *The Circuit*, tells the story of those younger years, as do his two picture books, *La Mariposa*, a Smithsonian Notable Book, and *The Christmas Gift*, an ALA Notable Book. He received both his master's degree and his Ph.D. from Columbia University and is now the Fay Boyle Professor of Modern Languages and Literatures and director of the ethnic studies program at Santa Clara University. He lives in Santa Clara, California, with his wife and three children.